To Lorraine

Our best snacks!

Jean Paré

most
loved
cookies

Pictured on front cover:
Decadent Chocolate Chippers, page 16

Pictured on back cover:
Top: Shortbread Pinwheels, page 28
Bottom right: Checkerboard Shortbread, page 28
Bottom left: Cloverleaf Shortbread, page 28

First Printing November 2005

Library and Archives Canada Cataloguing in Publication
Paré, Jean, date
Most loved cookies / Jean Paré.
(Most loved recipe collection)
Includes index.
ISBN 1-896891-67-5
1. Desserts. I. Title. II. Series: Paré, Jean, date. Most loved recipe collection.
TX772.P28 2005   641.8'654   C2005-901670-1

Published by
Company's Coming Publishing Limited
2311 – 96 Street
Edmonton, Alberta, Canada T6N 1G3
Tel: 780-450-6223   Fax: 780-450-1857
www.companyscoming.com

Company's Coming is a registered trademark owned by
Company's Coming Publishing Limited

Printed in China

We gratefully acknowledge the following suppliers for their generous support of our Test Kitchen and Photo Studio:

Corelle®
Hamilton Beach® Canada
Lagostina®
Proctor Silex® Canada
Tupperware®

Our special thanks to the following businesses for providing extensive props for photography:

A Taste of Provence
Anchor Hocking Canada
Browne & Co.
Canhome Global
Casa Bugatti
Cherison Enterprises Inc.
Corelle®
Danesco Inc.
Emile Henry
Island Pottery Inc.
Klass Works
La Cache
Linens 'N Things
Mikasa Home Store
Out of the Fire Studio
Pfaltzgraff Canada
Pier 1 Imports
Stokes

Pictured from left: Black Forest Cookies, page 78; Gingersnaps, page 62; Jam Jams, page 42; Chocolate Crinkles, page 64.

table of contents

the Company's Coming story

"never share a recipe you wouldn't use yourself"

Jean Paré (pronounced "Perry") grew up understanding that the combination of family, friends and home cooking is the best recipe for a good life. From her mother, she learned to appreciate good cooking, while her father praised even her earliest attempts in the kitchen. When Jean left home, she took with her many acquired family recipes, a love of cooking and an intriguing desire to read recipe books like novels!

In 1963, when her four children had all reached school age, Jean volunteered to cater the 50th Anniversary of the Vermilion School of Agriculture, now Lakeland College, in Alberta, Canada. Working out of her home, Jean prepared a dinner for over 1,000 people which launched a flourishing catering operation that continued for over eighteen years. During that time, she was provided with countless opportunities to test new ideas with immediate feedback—resulting in empty plates and contented customers! Whether preparing cocktail sandwiches for a house party or serving a hot meal for 1,500 people, Jean Paré earned a reputation for good food, courteous service and reasonable prices.

As requests for her recipes mounted, Jean was often asked the question, "Why don't you write a cookbook?" Jean responded by teaming up with her son, Grant Lovig, in the fall of 1980 to form Company's Coming Publishing Limited. The publication of the first Company's Coming cookbook on April 14, 1981 marked the debut of what would soon become one of the world's most popular cookbook series.

The company has grown since those early days when Jean worked from a spare bedroom in her home. Today she leads a team of writers and testers in the development of new recipes. Under the guidance of Jean's daughter, Gail Lovig, Company's Coming cookbooks are now distributed throughout Canada, in addition to the United States and numerous overseas markets. Rounding off three generations is Jean's granddaughter (Grant's daughter), Amanda Jean Lovig, who looks after publicity and arranges personal appearances for her grandmother.

Bestsellers many times over in English, Company's Coming cookbooks have also been published in French and Spanish. Familiar and trusted in home kitchens around the world, Company's Coming cookbooks are offered in a variety of formats. Highly regarded as kitchen workbooks, the softcover Original Series, with its lay-flat plastic comb binding, is still the favourite with readers.

Jean Paré's approach to cooking has always called for *quick and easy recipes* using *everyday ingredients*. Even when travelling, she is constantly on the lookout for new ideas to share with her readers. At home, she can usually be found researching and writing recipes, or helping in the company's test kitchen. Jean continues to gain new supporters by adhering to what she calls The Golden Rule of Cooking: *"Never share a recipe you wouldn't use yourself."* It's an approach that has worked—*millions of times over!*

foreword

Cookies have been a part of the human experience for centuries. When Columbus sailed the ocean blue, he likely ate a cookie or two! Hardtack, made of unleavened flour and water, was dried to make a brittle, cracker-like "ship's biscuit." These biscuits stayed fresh for months and provided sustenance for sailors on long voyages. Over time, and quite by accident, the sweet biscuit we know today as the "cookie" evolved. Early bakers used small amounts of cake batter to test their oven's temperature. These small test cakes became known as "cookies." The rest, as they say, is history—cookies have been a favourite treat around the world ever since.

The first North American cookies were simple shortbread and butter cookies. As trade developed, ingredients such as coconut, nuts and chocolate were added. Modern conveniences and food processing methods led to the popularity of icebox cookies and cookies made with breakfast cereals. Ruth Wakefield of Massachusetts is credited with inventing the chocolate chip cookie at her Toll House Inn. She cut up a bar of semi-sweet chocolate and stirred the bits into her cookie dough, assuming they would melt during baking. Instead, the bits remained intact and the chocolate chip cookie was born—now one of North America's most-loved cookies!

Cookies are known around the world as biscuits, keks, teacakes and biscotti, and everyone has a favourite. We've baked dozens of cookies over the years and discovered many of our own favourites. We're pleased to present them to you in *Most Loved Cookies*. From everyday sweets to special occasion treats, you'll find a delightful assortment of drop, refrigerator, cut-out, shaped, pressed and no-bake treats in *Most Loved Cookies*, along with a variety of helpful tips and information. Let your family choose their favourites and make cookie history in your own kitchen.

Enjoy!

Jean Paré

nutrition information

Each recipe is analyzed using the most current version of the Canadian Nutrient File from Health Canada, which is based on the United States Department of Agriculture (USDA) Nutrient Database.

- If more than one ingredient is listed (such as "hard margarine or butter"), or if a range is given (1 – 2 tsp., 5 – 10 mL), only the first ingredient or first amount is analyzed.

- For meat, poultry and fish, the serving size per person is based on the recommended 4 oz. (113 g) uncooked weight (without bone), which is 2 – 3 oz. (57 – 85 g) cooked weight (without bone)— approximately the size of a deck of playing cards.

- Milk used is 1% M.F. (milk fat), unless otherwise stated.

- Cooking oil used is canola oil, unless otherwise stated.

- Ingredients indicating "sprinkle," "optional," or "for garnish" are not included in the nutrition information.

Margaret Ng, B.Sc. (Hon), M.A.
Registered Dietitian

No added spices—just plain good! These cookies are filled with fibre and flavour. Keep your cookie jar well-stocked with these tasty treats. Your family will be coming back for more.

tip

To make drop cookies or balls that are uniform in size, use a small, self-clearing ice cream scoop.

Best Drop Cookies

Hard margarine (or butter), softened	1 cup	250 mL
Brown sugar, packed	1 1/2 cups	375 mL
Large eggs	2	2
Vanilla	1 tsp.	5 mL
All-purpose flour	2 cups	500 mL
Baking soda	1 tsp.	5 mL
Chopped pitted dates	1 lb.	454 g
Quick-cooking rolled oats (not instant)	1 cup	250 mL
Medium unsweetened coconut	1/2 cup	125 mL
Chopped walnuts	1/2 cup	125 mL
Quartered glazed cherries (optional)	1/2 cup	125 mL

Cream margarine and brown sugar in large bowl. Add eggs 1 at a time, beating well after each addition. Add vanilla. Beat until smooth.

Combine flour and baking soda in small bowl. Add to margarine mixture in 2 additions, mixing well after each addition until no dry flour remains.

Add remaining 5 ingredients. Mix well. Drop, using 1 1/2 tbsp. (25 mL) for each, about 2 inches (5 cm) apart onto greased cookie sheets. Bake in 350°F (175°C) oven for 10 to 12 minutes until golden. Remove to wire racks to cool. Makes about 5 dozen (60) cookies.

1 cookie: 109 Calories; 4.7 g Total Fat (2.4 g Mono, 0.8 g Poly, 1.2 g Sat); 7 mg Cholesterol; 16 g Carbohydrate; 1 g Fibre; 1 g Protein; 64 mg Sodium

Pictured on page 7.

An old favourite. These cookies get their name because they taste even better if they're hidden for a day or two after baking. Good luck—their spicy aroma is sure to bring any hermit out of hiding!

Hermits

Hard margarine (or butter), softened	1 cup	250 mL
Brown sugar, packed	1 1/2 cups	375 mL
Large eggs	3	3
Vanilla	1 tsp.	5 mL
All-purpose flour	3 cups	750 mL
Baking powder	1 tsp.	5 mL
Baking soda	1 tsp.	5 mL
Ground cinnamon	1 tsp.	5 mL
Salt	1/2 tsp.	2 mL
Ground nutmeg	1/2 tsp.	2 mL
Ground allspice	1/4 tsp.	1 mL
Raisins	1 cup	250 mL
Chopped pitted dates	1 cup	250 mL
Chopped walnuts (or your favourite nuts)	2/3 cup	150 mL

Cream margarine and brown sugar in large bowl. Add eggs 1 at a time, beating well after each addition. Add vanilla. Beat until smooth.

Combine next 7 ingredients in medium bowl. Add to margarine mixture in 3 additions, mixing well after each addition until no dry flour remains.

Add remaining 3 ingredients. Mix well. Drop, using 1 1/2 tbsp. (25 mL) for each, about 2 inches (5 cm) apart onto greased cookie sheets. Bake in 375°F (190°C) oven for 6 to 8 minutes until golden. Let stand for 5 minutes. Remove to wire racks to cool. Makes about 4 dozen (48) cookies.

1 cookie: 130 Calories; 5.5 g Total Fat (3 g Mono, 1.2 g Poly, 1 g Sat); 13 mg Cholesterol; 19 g Carbohydrate; 1 g Fibre; 2 g Protein; 114 mg Sodium

Pictured on page 9.

Kids of all ages are sure to love these. Keep them in the cookie jar for all your little pumpkins!

about cloves

Cloves are the dried flower buds of the tropical clove evergreen tree. In cookies and baked goods, ground cloves have a pungent aroma reminiscent of Christmas, but are good any time of the year.

Pumpkin Cookies

Hard margarine (or butter), softened	1/2 cup	125 mL
Brown sugar, packed	1 1/4 cups	300 mL
Large eggs	2	2
Canned pure pumpkin (no spices)	1 cup	250 mL
Vanilla	1 tsp.	5 mL
All-purpose flour	2 cups	500 mL
Baking powder	4 tsp.	20 mL
Salt	1/2 tsp.	2 mL
Ground cinnamon	1/2 tsp.	2 mL
Ground nutmeg	1/2 tsp.	2 mL
Ground cloves	1/4 tsp.	1 mL
Ground ginger	1/4 tsp.	1 mL
Raisins (or semi-sweet chocolate chips)	1 cup	250 mL
Chopped walnuts (or your favourite nuts)	1 cup	250 mL

Cream margarine and brown sugar in large bowl. Add eggs 1 at a time, beating well after each addition. Add pumpkin and vanilla. Beat until smooth.

Combine next 7 ingredients in small bowl. Add to margarine mixture in 2 additions, mixing well after each addition until no dry flour remains.

Add raisins and walnuts. Mix well. Drop, using 1 1/2 tbsp. (25 mL) for each, about 2 inches (5 cm) apart onto greased cookie sheets. Bake in 375°F (190°C) oven for about 15 minutes until golden. Let stand on cookie sheets for 5 minutes before removing to wire racks to cool. Makes about 4 dozen (48) cookies.

1 cookie: 93 Calories; 3.9 g Total Fat (1.8 g Mono, 1.3 g Poly, 0.6 g Sat); 9 mg Cholesterol; 14 g Carbohydrate; 1 g Fibre; 2 g Protein; 85 mg Sodium

Pictured on page 13.

Spicy Dads

Hard margarine (or butter), softened	1 cup	250 mL
Granulated sugar	1 cup	250 mL
Brown sugar, packed	1/2 cup	125 mL
Large egg	1	1
Fancy (mild) molasses	2 tbsp.	30 mL
Vanilla	1 tsp.	5 mL
All-purpose flour	1 1/2 cups	375 mL
Baking powder	1 tsp.	5 mL
Baking soda	1 tsp.	5 mL
Ground cinnamon	1 tsp.	5 mL
Ground nutmeg	1 tsp.	5 mL
Ground allspice	1 tsp.	5 mL
Quick-cooking rolled oats (not instant)	1 1/2 cups	375 mL
Medium unsweetened coconut	1 cup	250 mL

Cream margarine and both sugars in large bowl. Add egg. Beat well. Add molasses and vanilla. Beat until smooth.

Combine next 6 ingredients in small bowl. Add to margarine mixture in 2 additions, mixing well after each addition until no dry flour remains.

Add rolled oats and coconut. Mix well. Drop, using 1 tbsp. (15 mL) for each, about 2 inches (5 cm) apart onto greased cookie sheets. Flatten slightly. Bake in 300°F (150°C) oven for about 12 minutes until golden. Let stand on cookie sheets for 5 minutes before removing to wire racks to cool. Makes about 5 dozen (60) cookies.

1 cookie: 86 Calories; 4.6 g Total Fat (2.2 g Mono, 0.4 g Poly, 1.6 g Sat); 4 mg Cholesterol; 11 g Carbohydrate; trace Fibre; 1 g Protein; 68 mg Sodium

Pictured on page 13.

A spicier version of the commercial kind. Always good. Not only for Dad—the kids will love them, too!

about allspice

Did you know that allspice is a berry from a tree? It's called allspice because it tastes like a blend of cinnamon, nutmeg and cloves.

The enticing aroma of these carrot cookies wafting through the house will lead everyone by the nose to see what's up!

carrot ginger cookies

Crystallized ginger adds a sweet, spicy flavour to cookies. Use sparingly—it has quite a bite! In this recipe, add 1/4 cup (60 mL) minced crystallized ginger with the rolled oats and raisins.

Carrot Cookies

Hard margarine (or butter), softened	1/2 cup	125 mL
Granulated sugar	1 cup	250 mL
Large egg	1	1
Cooked mashed carrot	1 cup	250 mL
Milk	1/3 cup	75 mL
Vanilla	1 tsp.	5 mL
All-purpose flour	2 cups	500 mL
Baking powder	2 tsp.	10 mL
Ground cinnamon	1 tsp.	5 mL
Salt	1/4 tsp.	1 mL
Quick-cooking rolled oats (not instant)	2 cups	500 mL
Raisins	1 cup	250 mL
ORANGE ICING		
Icing (confectioner's) sugar	2 1/2 cups	625 mL
Hard margarine (or butter), softened	1/3 cup	75 mL
Orange juice	2 tbsp.	30 mL
Grated orange zest	1 1/2 tbsp.	25 mL

Cream margarine and sugar in large bowl. Add egg. Beat well. Add carrot, milk and vanilla. Beat until smooth.

Combine next 4 ingredients in small bowl. Add to margarine mixture in 2 additions, mixing well after each addition until no dry flour remains.

Add rolled oats and raisins. Mix well. Drop, using 1 tbsp. (15 mL) for each, about 2 inches (5 cm) apart onto greased cookie sheets. Bake in 375°F (190°C) oven for 12 to 15 minutes until golden. Remove to wire racks to cool completely.

Orange Icing: Beat all 4 ingredients in medium bowl, adding more icing sugar or orange juice if necessary until spreading consistency. Makes about 1 1/2 cups (375 mL) icing. Spread about 1 tbsp. (15 mL) icing on top of each cookie. Makes about 5 dozen (60) cookies.

1 cookie: 100 Calories; 3.1 g Total Fat (1.9 g Mono, 0.4 g Poly, 0.6 g Sat); 4 mg Cholesterol; 7 g Carbohydrate; 1 g Fibre; 1 g Protein; 59 mg Sodium

Pictured on page 13.

Top left: Pumpkin Cookies, page 10
Top right: Spicy Dads, page 11
Bottom: Carrot Cookies, above

For chocolate fans! Walnuts give these soft cookies a bit of pizzazz, but they're just as good without them.

note

To make sour milk, measure 1 tsp. (5 mL) white vinegar or lemon juice into a 1 cup (250 mL) liquid measure. Add enough milk to make 1/3 cup (75 mL). Stir. Let stand for 1 minute.

Chocolate Softies

Hard margarine (or butter), softened	1/2 cup	125 mL
Granulated sugar	1 cup	250 mL
Large egg	1	1
Unsweetened chocolate baking squares (1 oz., 28 g, each), chopped	2	2
Sour milk (see Note)	1/3 cup	75 mL
Vanilla	1 tsp.	5 mL
All-purpose flour	1 3/4 cups	425 mL
Baking soda	1/2 tsp.	2 mL
Salt	1/2 tsp.	2 mL
Chopped walnuts (optional)	1/2 cup	125 mL
CHOCOLATE ICING		
Icing (confectioner's) sugar	1 1/4 cups	300 mL
Cocoa, sifted if lumpy	1/3 cup	75 mL
Hard margarine (or butter), softened	3 tbsp.	50 mL
Hot strong prepared coffee (or water)	1 1/2 tbsp.	25 mL

Cream margarine and sugar in large bowl. Add egg. Beat well.

Heat chocolate in small heavy saucepan on lowest heat, stirring often until almost melted. Do not overheat. Remove from heat. Stir until smooth. Add to margarine mixture. Add sour milk and vanilla. Stir well.

Combine flour, baking soda and salt in small bowl. Add to chocolate mixture in 2 additions, mixing well after each addition until no dry flour remains.

Add walnuts. Mix well. Drop, using 1 tbsp. (15 mL) for each, about 2 inches (5 cm) apart onto ungreased cookie sheets. Bake in 350°F (175°C) oven for 10 to 12 minutes until firm. Let stand on cookie sheets for 5 minutes before removing to wire racks to cool completely.

Chocolate Icing: Beat all 4 ingredients in medium bowl, adding more icing sugar or coffee if necessary until spreading consistency. Makes about 2 cups (500 mL) icing. Spread about 2 tsp. (10 mL) icing on top of each cookie. Makes about 4 dozen (48) cookies.

1 cookie: 82 Calories; 3.6 g Total Fat (2.1 g Mono, 0.3 g Poly, 1.1 g Sat); 5 mg Cholesterol; 12 g Carbohydrate; 1 g Fibre; 1 g Protein; 73 mg Sodium

Pictured on page 15.

Dipper some Chippers in a glass of cold milk!

decadent chocolate chippers

Turn Chocolate Chippers into decadent dunkers! Omit the chocolate chips, use 3 cups (750 mL) chocolate chunks, and increase the walnuts to 2 cups (500 mL).

Pictured on front cover.

chipper pizza

Make cookie dough according to the recipe. Press dough evenly in greased 12 inch (30 cm) pizza pan. Sprinkle with:

1/2 cup (125 mL) candy-coated chocolate candies (such as Smarties or M & M's)

1/3 cup (75 mL) butterscotch chips

1/4 cup (60 mL) cornflakes cereal

1/4 cup (60 mL) peanuts

2 tbsp. (30 mL) medium sweetened coconut

1 tbsp. (15 mL) toffee bits (such as Skor or Heath Bar)

Bake in 350°F (175°C) oven for 12 to 15 minutes until golden.

Pictured on page 17.

Chocolate Chippers

Hard margarine (or butter), softened	1 cup	250 mL
Brown sugar, packed	1 1/2 cups	375 mL
Large eggs	2	2
Vanilla	1 tsp.	5 mL
All-purpose flour	2 cups	500 mL
Cornstarch	1/4 cup	60 mL
Baking soda	1 tsp.	5 mL
Salt	3/4 tsp.	4 mL
Semi-sweet chocolate chips	2 cups	500 mL
Coarsely chopped walnuts (optional)	1 cup	250 mL

Cream margarine and brown sugar in large bowl. Add eggs 1 at a time, beating well after each addition. Add vanilla. Beat until smooth.

Combine next 4 ingredients in small bowl. Add to margarine mixture in 2 additions, mixing well after each addition until no dry flour remains.

Add chocolate chips and walnuts. Mix well. Drop, using 1 1/2 tbsp. (25 mL) for each, about 2 inches (5 cm) apart onto greased cookie sheets. Bake in 350°F (175°C) oven for 10 to 15 minutes until golden. Let stand on cookie sheets for 5 minutes before removing to wire racks to cool. Makes about 3 dozen (36) cookies.

1 cookie: 166 Calories; 8.7 g Total Fat (4.6 g Mono, 0.7 g Poly, 3 g Sat); 12 mg Cholesterol; 22 g Carbohydrate; 1 g Fibre; 2 g Protein; 157 mg Sodium

Pictured on page 17.

Top: Chipper Pizza, this page
Bottom: Chocolate Chippers, above

For cherry lovers—a soft, golden cookie filled with cherries, dates, nuts and coconut.

Cherry Snacks

Hard margarine (or butter), softened	1 cup	250 mL
Granulated sugar	3/4 cup	175 mL
All-purpose flour	2 cups	500 mL
Salt	1/2 tsp.	2 mL
Boiling water	1/4 cup	60 mL
Baking soda	1 tsp.	5 mL
Chopped pitted dates	1 cup	250 mL
Chopped walnuts	1 cup	250 mL
Chopped glazed cherries	1 cup	250 mL
Medium unsweetened coconut	3/4 cup	175 mL

Cream margarine and sugar in large bowl. Add flour and salt. Mix until no dry flour remains.

Stir boiling water into baking soda in small bowl until dissolved. Add to margarine mixture. Stir well.

Add remaining 4 ingredients. Mix well. Drop, using 1 tbsp. (15 mL) for each, about 2 inches (5 cm) apart onto greased cookie sheets. Bake in 350°F (175°C) oven for 12 to 15 minutes until golden. Remove to wire racks to cool. Makes about 4 dozen (48) cookies.

1 cookie: 119 Calories; 6.6 g Total Fat (3 g Mono, 1.5 g Poly, 1.8 g Sat); 0 mg Cholesterol; 15 g Carbohydrate; 1 g Fibre; 1 g Protein; 100 mg Sodium

Pictured on pages 20/21.

Make a double batch and keep some in the freezer. They're always good for rounding out a lunch box, and equally appreciated at snack time after school.

Oatmeal Raisin Cookies

Hard margarine (or butter), softened	1 cup	250 mL
Brown sugar, packed	1 cup	250 mL
Large egg	1	1
Vanilla	1 tsp.	5 mL
All-purpose flour	1 1/2 cups	375 mL
Baking soda	1 tsp.	5 mL
Salt	1/4 tsp.	1 mL
Quick-cooking rolled oats (not instant)	1 1/4 cups	300 mL
Raisins	1 cup	250 mL

(continued on next page)

Cream margarine and brown sugar in large bowl. Add egg. Beat well. Add vanilla. Beat until smooth.

Combine flour, baking soda and salt in small bowl. Add to margarine mixture in 2 additions, mixing well after each addition until no dry flour remains.

Add rolled oats and raisins. Mix well. Drop, using 1 tbsp. (15 mL) for each, about 2 inches (5 cm) apart onto greased cookie sheets. Bake in 350°F (175°C) oven for 8 to 10 minutes until golden. Let stand on cookie sheets for 5 minutes before removing to wire racks to cool. Makes about 3 1/2 dozen (42) cookies.

1 cookie: 104 Calories; 5 g Total Fat (3.1 g Mono, 0.6 g Poly, 1 g Sat); 5 mg Cholesterol; 14 g Carbohydrate; 1 g Fibre; 1 g Protein; 103 mg Sodium

Pictured on page 20.

tip
To prevent cookies from sticking together during freezing, layer completely cooled cookies between sheets of waxed paper in an airtight container. Freeze for up to 3 months.

Chocolate Nuggets

Semi-sweet chocolate chips	2 cups	500 mL
Can of sweetened condensed milk	11 oz.	300 mL
Hard margarine (or butter)	1/4 cup	60 mL
Granulated sugar	1/4 cup	60 mL
Vanilla	1 tsp.	5 mL
All-purpose flour	1 cup	250 mL
Chopped walnuts (or your favourite nuts), optional	1/2 cup	125 mL

Tasty chocolate morsels with a brownie-like texture. Yum!

Heat first 5 ingredients in heavy medium saucepan on lowest heat, stirring often until chocolate chips are almost melted. Do not overheat. Remove from heat. Stir until smooth.

Add flour and walnuts. Mix until no dry flour remains. Drop, using 1 tsp. (5 mL) for each, about 2 inches (5 cm) apart onto greased cookie sheets. Bake in 350°F (175°C) oven for 10 to 12 minutes until dry. Cookies will be soft. Let stand on cookie sheets for 5 minutes before removing to wire racks to cool. Makes about 6 dozen (72) cookies.

1 cookie: 57 Calories; 2.6 g Total Fat (1.1 g Mono, 0.1 g Poly, 1.3 g Sat); 2 mg Cholesterol; 8 g Carbohydrate; trace Fibre; 1 g Protein; 15 mg Sodium

Pictured on page 21.

Photo legend, next page
Top left: Oatmeal Raisin Cookies, page 18
Top right: Cherry Snacks, page 18
Bottom right: Chocolate Nuggets, this page
Bottom left: Gumdrop Cookies, page 22

Goody, goody, gumdrops! Dotted with colourful candy, these won't last long.

tip

If your cookies are brown on the bottom but not cooked through, move the cookie sheet to a higher rack in the oven, or add insulation by slipping a second cookie sheet under the first.

Gumdrop Cookies

Hard margarine (or butter), softened	1 cup	250 mL
Brown sugar, packed	1 cup	250 mL
Granulated sugar	1/4 cup	60 mL
Large eggs	2	2
Vanilla	1 tsp.	5 mL
All-purpose flour	1 1/2 cups	375 mL
Baking powder	1 tsp.	5 mL
Baking soda	1/2 tsp.	2 mL
Salt	1/2 tsp.	2 mL
Quick-cooking rolled oats (not instant)	1 cup	250 mL
Chopped gumdrops (no black)	1 cup	250 mL
Chopped nuts (your favourite), optional	1/2 cup	125 mL

Cream margarine and both sugars in large bowl. Add eggs 1 at a time, beating well after each addition. Add vanilla. Beat until smooth.

Combine next 4 ingredients in small bowl. Add to margarine mixture in 2 additions, mixing well after each addition until no dry flour remains.

Add remaining 3 ingredients. Mix well. Drop, using 1 tbsp. (15 mL) for each, about 2 inches (5 cm) apart onto ungreased cookie sheets. Bake in 350°F (175°C) oven for 12 to 14 minutes until golden. Let stand on cookie sheets for 5 minutes before removing to wire racks to cool. Makes about 4 dozen (48) cookies.

1 cookie: 101 Calories; 4.4 g Total Fat (2.8 g Mono, 0.5 g Poly, 0.9 g Sat); 9 mg Cholesterol; 15 g Carbohydrate; trace Fibre; 1 g Protein; 99 mg Sodium

Pictured on page 20.

The perfect macaroon—sweet and chewy in the middle, crispy on the outside. Drizzle these with melted chocolate for an extra-special treat.

Macaroons

Granulated sugar	3/4 cup	175 mL
Cornstarch	2 tbsp.	30 mL
Salt	1/8 tsp.	0.5 mL
Egg whites (large)	3	3
Shredded (long thread) coconut	4 cups	1 L

(continued on next page)

Combine sugar, cornstarch and salt in small bowl.

Beat egg whites on high in top of double boiler or large heatproof bowl for about 5 minutes until stiff, dry peaks form. Place over boiling water in double boiler or medium saucepan. Add sugar mixture in 3 additions, beating on medium-high for about 1 minute until smooth and glossy. Cook for about 6 minutes, without stirring, until dry crust forms around edge.

Fold meringue into coconut in large bowl until well combined. Drop, using 2 tsp. (10 mL) for each, about 2 inches (5 cm) apart onto greased cookie sheets. Bake in 350°F (175°C) oven for about 12 minutes until golden. Let stand on cookie sheets for 5 minutes before removing to wire racks to cool. Makes about 4 dozen (48) macaroons.

1 macaroon: 67 Calories; 5.1 g Total Fat (0.2 g Mono, 0.1 g Poly, 4.5 g Sat); 0 mg Cholesterol; 6 g Carbohydrate; trace Fibre; 1 g Protein; 13 mg Sodium

Pictured below.

Top: Macaroons, page 22
Bottom: White Chip Cookies, page 24

A new chip off the old block. White chocolate chips peek through this dark chocolate cookie. Scrumptious.

White Chip Cookies

Hard margarine (or butter), softened	1/2 cup	125 mL
Brown sugar, packed	1 cup	250 mL
Cocoa, sifted if lumpy	1/2 cup	125 mL
Large egg	1	1
Vanilla	1 tsp.	5 mL
All-purpose flour	1 cup	250 mL
Baking soda	1/2 tsp.	2 mL
Salt	1/2 tsp.	2 mL
White chocolate chips	1 cup	250 mL
Chopped walnuts (or pecans), optional	3/4 cup	175 mL

Cream margarine and brown sugar in large bowl. Add cocoa. Beat well. Add egg and vanilla. Beat until smooth.

Combine flour, baking soda and salt in small bowl. Add to margarine mixture. Mix until no dry flour remains.

Add white chocolate chips and walnuts. Mix well. Drop, using 1 tbsp. (15 mL) for each, about 2 inches (5 cm) apart onto greased cookie sheets. Flatten slightly. Bake in 350ºF (175ºC) oven for 10 to 12 minutes until firm. Let stand on cookie sheets for 5 minutes before removing to wire racks to cool. Makes about 3 dozen (36) cookies.

1 cookie: 94 Calories; 4.6 g Total Fat (2.3 g Mono, 0.4 g Poly, 1.6 g Sat); 7 mg Cholesterol; 13 g Carbohydrate; 1 g Fibre; 1 g Protein; 91 mg Sodium

Pictured on page 23.

The goodness of bran and nuts in a not-too-sweet treat. Good with or without cinnamon.

Bran Cereal Cookies

Hard margarine (or butter), softened	1 cup	250 mL
Granulated sugar	1 cup	250 mL
Large eggs	2	2
Vanilla	1 1/2 tsp.	7 mL

(continued on next page)

All-purpose flour	1 1/2 cups	375 mL
Baking soda	1 tsp.	5 mL
Ground cinnamon (optional)	1 tsp.	5 mL
Salt	1/2 tsp.	2 mL
All-bran cereal	1 1/2 cups	375 mL
Chopped walnuts (or your favourite nuts)	1 cup	250 mL

tip

To soften cookies, place them in an airtight container with a quarter of a fresh apple for 24 hours. The cookies will become moist and have a subtle apple flavour.

Cream margarine and sugar in large bowl. Add eggs 1 at a time, beating well after each addition. Add vanilla. Beat until smooth.

Combine next 4 ingredients in small bowl. Add to margarine mixture in 2 additions, mixing well after each addition until no dry flour remains.

Add cereal and walnuts. Mix well. Drop, using 1 tbsp. (15 mL) for each, about 2 inches (5 cm) apart onto greased cookie sheets. Bake in 375°F (190°C) oven for 12 to 14 minutes until golden. Remove to wire racks to cool. Makes about 4 1/2 dozen (54) cookies.

1 cookie: 83 Calories; 5.2 g Total Fat (2.7 g Mono, 1.3 g Poly, 0.9 g Sat); 8 mg Cholesterol; 9 g Carbohydrate; 1 g Fibre; 1 g Protein; 108 mg Sodium

Pictured below.

Cheery cherry cookies are so hard to resist!

note

To toast nuts, spread them evenly in an ungreased shallow pan. Bake in a 350ºF (175ºC) oven for 5 to 10 minutes, stirring or shaking often, until desired doneness.

cherry pecan butter cookies

Omit the slivered almonds. Use the same amount of pecan pieces.

Cherry Almond Butter Cookies

Butter (not margarine), softened	2 cups	500 mL
Granulated sugar	1 1/2 cups	375 mL
Large egg	1	1
Vanilla	2 tsp.	10 mL
All-purpose flour	5 cups	1.25 L
Baking powder	2 tsp.	10 mL
Salt	1/2 tsp.	2 mL
Dried cherries	1 1/3 cups	325 mL
Slivered almonds, toasted (see Note)	1 cup	250 mL

Cream butter and sugar in large bowl. Add egg. Beat well. Add vanilla. Beat until smooth.

Combine flour, baking powder and salt in medium bowl. Add to butter mixture in 3 additions, mixing well after each addition until no dry flour remains.

Add cherries. Mix well. Divide dough into 3 equal portions. Shape each portion into 8 inch (20 cm) long log. Wrap each log with waxed paper. Chill for at least 6 hours or overnight. Discard waxed paper from 1 log. Cut into 1/3 inch (1 cm) slices. Arrange about 2 inches (5 cm) apart on greased cookie sheets.

Gently press 2 or 3 almond slivers in decorative pattern on top of each slice. Bake in 350ºF (175ºC) oven for about 10 minutes until just golden. Let stand on cookie sheets for 5 minutes before removing to wire racks to cool. Repeat with remaining logs and almond slivers. Makes about 6 dozen (72) cookies.

1 cookie: 119 Calories; 6.7 g Total Fat (2.3 g Mono, 0.5 g Poly, 3.5 g Sat); 18 mg Cholesterol; 14 g Carbohydrate; 1 g Fibre; 2 g Protein; 83 mg Sodium

Pictured on page 27.

Buttery shortbread gets a chocolate spin. Prepare the dough one day and bake it the next.

checkerboard shortbread

Divide chocolate dough into 2 equal portions. Repeat with white dough. Shape each portion into 12 inch (30 cm) long rope. Position all 4 ropes as shown in Diagram B. Wrap together with waxed paper. Chill, cut and bake as directed.

Pictured on page 29 and on back cover.

cloverleaf shortbread

Omit cocoa. Divide entire amount of dough into 3 equal portions. Colour 1 portion yellow, 1 pink and 1 green with drops of liquid food colouring. Shape each portion into 12 inch (30 cm) long rope. Position all 3 ropes as shown in Diagram C. Wrap together with waxed paper. Chill, cut and bake as directed.

Pictured on page 29 and on back cover.

Shortbread Pinwheels

Butter (not margarine), softened	1 cup	250 mL
Icing (confectioner's) sugar	2/3 cup	150 mL
Vanilla	1/2 tsp.	2 mL
All-purpose flour	2 cups	500 mL
Cocoa, sifted if lumpy	1/4 cup	60 mL

Beat butter, icing sugar and vanilla in medium bowl until smooth. Add flour in 2 additions, mixing well after each addition until no dry flour remains. Divide dough into 2 equal portions.

Add cocoa to 1 dough portion. Mix until evenly coloured. Roll out chocolate dough between 2 sheets of waxed paper to 7 x 12 inch (18 x 30 cm) rectangle. Repeat with remaining dough portion. Discard top sheet of waxed paper from both rectangles. Flip 1 rectangle onto the other, aligning edges of dough as evenly as possible. Discard top sheet of waxed paper. Roll up tightly from long side, jelly roll-style, using waxed paper as a guide (see Diagram A). Wrap with same sheet of waxed paper. Chill for at least 6 hours or overnight. Discard waxed paper. Cut into 1/3 inch (1 cm) slices. Arrange about 2 inches (5 cm) apart on ungreased cookie sheets. Bake in 350°F (175°C) oven for 10 to 12 minutes until firm. Let stand on cookie sheets for 5 minutes before removing to wire racks to cool. Makes about 3 dozen (36) cookies.

1 cookie: 85 Calories; 5.6 g Total Fat (1.6 g Mono, 0.2 g Poly, 3.4 g Sat); 15 mg Cholesterol; 8 g Carbohydrate; trace Fibre; 1 g Protein; 55 mg Sodium

Pictured on page 29 and on back cover.

Diagram A
(Pinwheel)

Diagram B
(Checkerboard)

Diagram C
(Cloverleaf)

Top: Shortbread Pinwheels, above
Bottom right: Checkerboard Shortbread, this page
Bottom left: Cloverleaf Shortbread, this page

Simply delicious. Makes a huge batch for stocking up the freezer.

an added touch

Drizzle melted butterscotch chips in a decorative pattern over the baked cookies.

Butterscotch Cookies

Hard margarine (or butter), softened	1 cup	250 mL
Brown sugar, packed	2 cups	500 mL
Large eggs	2	2
Vanilla	1 tsp.	5 mL
All-purpose flour	3 cups	750 mL
Baking soda	1 tsp.	5 mL
Chopped walnuts	1 cup	250 mL

Cream margarine and brown sugar in large bowl. Add eggs 1 at a time, beating well after each addition. Add vanilla. Beat until smooth.

Combine flour and baking soda in medium bowl. Add to margarine mixture in 3 additions, mixing well after each addition until no dry flour remains.

Add walnuts. Mix well. Divide dough into 4 equal portions. Shape each portion into 9 inch (22 cm) long log. Wrap each log with waxed paper. Chill for at least 6 hours or overnight. Discard waxed paper from 1 log. Cut into 1/4 inch (6 mm) slices. Arrange about 2 inches (5 cm) apart on ungreased cookie sheets. Bake in 350°F (175°C) oven for 8 to 10 minutes until golden. Let stand on cookie sheets for 5 minutes before removing to wire racks to cool. Repeat with remaining logs. Makes about 12 dozen (144) cookies.

1 cookie: 41 Calories; 2 g Total Fat (1 g Mono, 0.5 g Poly, 0.3 g Sat); 3 mg Cholesterol; 5 g Carbohydrate; trace Fibre; 1 g Protein; 27 mg Sodium

Pictured on page 31.

These pastry-like cookies topped with your favourite jam or marmalade are sure to please.

Cream Cheese Cookies

Hard margarine (or butter), softened	1/2 cup	125 mL
Granulated sugar	1/3 cup	75 mL
Cream cheese, softened	1/4 cup	60mL
Vanilla	1/2 tsp.	2 mL
All-purpose flour	1 cup	250 mL
Jam (or marmalade), your favourite, approximately	1 cup	250 mL

(continued on next page)

Cream margarine and sugar in medium bowl. Add cream cheese. Beat well. Add vanilla. Beat until smooth.

Add flour. Mix until no dry flour remains. Divide dough into 2 equal portions. Shape each portion into 5 inch (12.5 cm) long log. Wrap each log with waxed paper. Chill for at least 6 hours or overnight. Discard waxed paper from 1 log. Cut into 1/4 inch (6 mm) slices. Arrange about 2 inches (5 cm) apart on ungreased cookie sheets.

Spoon about 1 tsp. (5 mL) jam onto centre of each slice. Bake in 350°F (175°C) oven for 8 to 10 minutes until golden. Let stand on cookie sheets for 5 minutes before removing to wire racks to cool. Repeat with remaining log and jam. Makes about 3 dozen (36) cookies.

1 cookie: 74 Calories; 3.3 g Total Fat (1.9 g Mono, 0.3 g Poly, 0.9 g Sat); 2 mg Cholesterol; 11 g Carbohydrate; trace Fibre; 1 g Protein; 40 mg Sodium

Pictured below.

cream cheese crescents

Prepare dough as directed. Flatten logs slightly before wrapping and chilling. Roll out 1 portion on lightly floured surface to 8 x 10 inch (20 x 25 cm) rectangle. Cut into 2 inch (5 cm) squares. Spread jam onto each square, leaving 1/4 inch (6 mm) edge. Roll up diagonally from 1 corner toward opposite corner to enclose jam. Bend both ends slightly to form crescent shape. Bake as directed. Repeat with remaining dough and jam. Makes about 40 crescents.

Left: Butterscotch Cookies, page 30
Right: Cream Cheese Cookies, page 30

For peanut butter and jam fans. These crisp, golden cookies are perfect with a glass of cold milk.

PBJ Crisps

Hard margarine (or butter), softened	1/2 cup	125 mL
Granulated sugar	1/2 cup	125 mL
Smooth peanut butter	1/2 cup	125 mL
Raspberry jam	1/2 cup	125 mL
Large egg	1	1
Vanilla	1 tsp.	5 mL
All-purpose flour	2 1/2 cups	625 mL
Baking powder	1 1/2 tsp.	7 mL
Baking soda	1/2 tsp.	2 mL
Salt	1/2 tsp.	2 mL
Coarsely chopped peanuts	1/2 cup	125 mL

Cream margarine and sugar in large bowl. Add peanut butter and jam. Beat until well combined.

Add egg and vanilla. Beat until smooth.

Combine next 4 ingredients in medium bowl. Add to margarine mixture in 2 additions, mixing well after each addition until no dry flour remains.

Add peanuts. Mix well. Divide dough into 2 equal portions. Shape each portion into 8 inch (20 cm) long log. Wrap each log with waxed paper. Chill for at least 6 hours or overnight. Discard waxed paper from 1 log. Cut into 1/4 inch (6 mm) slices. Arrange about 2 inches (5 cm) apart on greased cookie sheets. Bake in 350°F (175°C) oven for about 12 minutes until golden. Let stand on cookie sheets for 5 minutes before removing to wire racks to cool. Repeat with remaining log. Makes about 5 dozen (60) cookies.

1 cookie: 69 Calories; 3.4 g Total Fat (1.9 g Mono, 0.7 g Poly, 0.7 g Sat); 4 mg Cholesterol; 8 g Carbohydrate; trace Fibre; 2 g Protein; 72 mg Sodium

Pictured on page 33.

An old favourite—lots of variations.

raspberry pinwheels

Prepare and roll out cookie dough as directed. Omit the date mixture. On each dough portion, spread 2 tbsp. (30 mL) raspberry jam, leaving 1/2 inch (12 mm) edge. Sprinkle 2 tbsp. (30 mL) shredded (long thread) coconut and 1 tbsp. (15 mL) finely chopped walnuts (or your favourite nuts) over jam. Roll up, jelly roll-style, and wrap with waxed paper. Chill, slice and bake as directed.

Pictured on page 35.

chocolate pinwheels

Prepare and roll out cookie dough as directed. Omit the date mixture. Heat 1/2 cup (125 mL) semi-sweet chocolate chips in a small heavy saucepan on lowest heat, stirring often until almost melted. Do not overheat. Remove from heat. Stir until smooth. On each dough portion, spread about 2 tbsp. (30 mL) chocolate, leaving 1/2 inch (12 mm) edge. Roll up, jelly roll-style, and wrap with waxed paper. Chill until chocolate is set. Bring rolls to room temperature before slicing and baking as directed.

Pictured on page 35.

Date Pinwheels

Chopped pitted dates	1 lb.	454 g
Granulated sugar	1/2 cup	125 mL
Water	1/3 cup	75 mL
Finely chopped walnuts	2/3 cup	150 mL
Hard margarine (or butter), softened	1 cup	250 mL
Brown sugar, packed	1 cup	250 mL
Granulated sugar	1 cup	250 mL
Large eggs	2	2
Vanilla	2 tsp.	10 mL
All-purpose flour	3 1/2 cups	875 mL
Baking soda	1 tsp.	5 mL
Salt	1/2 tsp.	2 mL

Combine dates, first amount of granulated sugar and water in medium saucepan. Bring to a boil on medium. Reduce heat to medium-low. Simmer, uncovered, for about 10 minutes, stirring occasionally, adding more water if necessary while simmering, until dates are softened. Remove from heat. Add walnuts. Stir. Let stand for 10 minutes.

Cream margarine, brown sugar and second amount of granulated sugar in large bowl. Add eggs 1 at a time, beating well after each addition. Add vanilla. Beat until smooth.

Combine flour, baking soda and salt in medium bowl. Add to margarine mixture in 3 additions, mixing well after each addition until no dry flour remains. Divide dough into 4 equal portions. Roll out 1 portion between 2 sheets of waxed paper to 8 inch (20 cm) square. Discard top sheet of waxed paper. Spread about 1/4 of date mixture evenly on dough, leaving 1/2 inch (12 mm) edge. Roll up tightly, jelly roll-style, using waxed paper as a guide. Wrap with same sheet of waxed paper. Repeat with remaining dough portions and date mixture, wrapping each roll with waxed paper. Chill for at least 6 hours or overnight. Discard waxed paper from 1 roll. Cut into 1/4 inch (6 mm) slices. Arrange about 2 inches (5 cm) apart on greased cookie sheets. Bake in 375°F (190°C) oven for 8 to 10 minutes until golden. Let stand on cookie sheets for 5 minutes before removing to wire racks to cool. Repeat with remaining rolls. Makes about 10 1/2 dozen (126) pinwheels.

1 pinwheel: 59 Calories; 2.1 g Total Fat (1.1 g Mono, 0.4 g Poly, 0.4 g Sat); 3 mg Cholesterol; 10 g Carbohydrate; trace Fibre; 1 g Protein; 40 mg Sodium

Pictured on page 35.

Top: Raspberry Pinwheels, this page
Centre: Date Pinwheels, above
Bottom: Chocolate Pinwheels, this page

Deliciously crisp, with a lovely citrus glaze drizzled on top. A nice tea time cookie.

chocolate-dipped lemon cookies

Prepare and shape dough as directed. Slightly flatten both round logs to create squared logs. Chill, cut and bake as directed. Omit Lemon Glaze.

Heat 3 chopped 1 oz. (28 g) squares of semi-sweet chocolate in a small heavy saucepan on lowest heat, stirring often until chocolate is almost melted. Do not overheat. Remove from heat. Stir until smooth. Transfer to a small custard cup. Dip cookies halfway into chocolate. Place on a waxed paper-lined cookie sheet. Let stand until set.

Pictured on page 37.

Lemon Icebox Cookies

Hard margarine (or butter), softened	1 cup	250 mL
Granulated sugar	3/4 cup	175 mL
Large eggs	2	2
Grated lemon zest	1 tbsp.	15 mL
All-purpose flour	3 cups	750 mL
Baking powder	1/2 tsp.	2 mL
Salt	1/4 tsp.	1 mL
LEMON GLAZE		
Lemon juice	1 – 2 tbsp.	15 – 30 mL
Icing (confectioner's) sugar	1/2 cup	125 mL
Drop of yellow liquid food colouring (optional)	1	1

Cream margarine and sugar in large bowl. Add eggs 1 at a time, beating well after each addition. Add lemon zest. Beat until smooth.

Combine flour, baking powder and salt in medium bowl. Add to margarine mixture in 3 additions, mixing well after each addition until no dry flour remains. Divide dough into 2 equal portions. Shape each portion into 8 inch (20 cm) long log. Wrap each log with waxed paper. Chill for at least 6 hours or overnight. Discard waxed paper from 1 log. Cut into 1/4 inch (6 mm) slices. Arrange about 2 inches (5 cm) apart on ungreased cookie sheets. Bake in 375°F (190°C) oven for 7 to 10 minutes until golden. Let stand on cookie sheets for 5 minutes before removing to wire racks to cool completely. Repeat with remaining log.

Lemon Glaze: Stir lemon juice into icing sugar in small bowl, adding more lemon juice or icing sugar if necessary until pourable consistency. Add food colouring. Mix well. Makes 1/4 cup (60 mL) glaze. Spoon glaze into small resealable freezer bag, then snip tiny piece off corner. Drizzle glaze in decorative pattern over cookies. Let stand until set. Makes about 5 dozen (60) cookies.

1 cookie: 70 Calories; 3.5 g Total Fat (2.2 g Mono, 0.4 g Poly, 0.7 g Sat); 7 mg Cholesterol; 9 g Carbohydrate; trace Fibre; 1 g Protein; 53 mg Sodium

Pictured on page 37.

Left: Chocolate-Dipped Lemon Cookies, this page
Right: Lemon Icebox Cookies, above

Fill your kitchen with the enticing aroma of cinnamon. It's an irresistible invitation to come and taste these pretty cookies!

about cinnamon

Cinnamon comes from the inner bark of a tropical evergreen tree. As the bark dries, it twists into long, slender curls which are then cut into sticks or ground into powder. Its mild, lingering flavour is a favourite addition to cookies and other baked goods.

Cinnamon Roll Cookies

Hard margarine (or butter), softened	1 cup	250 mL
Granulated sugar	3/4 cup	175 mL
Block of cream cheese, softened	4 oz.	125 g
Large egg	1	1
Vanilla	1 tsp.	5 mL
All-purpose flour	2 1/4 cups	550 mL
Baking soda	1/2 tsp.	2 mL
Salt	1/4 tsp.	1 mL
Hard margarine (or butter), melted	1 tbsp.	15 mL
Brown sugar, packed	2 tbsp.	30 mL
Ground cinnamon	1/2 tsp.	2 mL

Cream first amount of margarine and granulated sugar in large bowl. Add cream cheese. Beat until well combined. Add egg and vanilla. Beat until smooth.

Combine flour, baking soda and salt in medium bowl. Add to margarine mixture in 2 additions, mixing well after each addition until no dry flour remains. Roll out dough between 2 sheets of waxed paper to 9 x 13 inch (22 x 33 cm) rectangle. Discard top sheet of waxed paper.

Brush second amount of margarine evenly on dough. Sprinkle brown sugar evenly over margarine. Sprinkle cinnamon evenly over top. Roll up tightly from long side, jelly roll-style, using waxed paper as a guide. Wrap with same sheet of waxed paper. Chill for at least 6 hours or overnight. Discard waxed paper. Cut into 1/4 inch (6 mm) slices. Arrange about 2 inches (5 cm) apart on greased cookie sheets. Bake in 350°F (175°C) oven for 10 to 12 minutes until golden. Let stand on cookie sheets for 5 minutes before removing to wire racks to cool. Makes about 4 dozen (48) cookies.

1 roll: 87 Calories; 5.3 g Total Fat (3.1 g Mono, 0.5 g Poly, 1.5 g Sat); 7 mg Cholesterol; 9 g Carbohydrate; trace Fibre; 1 g Protein; 85 mg Sodium

Pictured on page 39.

Lovely for lemon lovers.
Perfect for parties.

Lemon Cookies

Ingredient	Imperial	Metric
Hard margarine (or butter), softened	1/2 cup	125 mL
Granulated sugar	1/2 cup	125 mL
Large egg	1	1
Sweetened condensed milk	2/3 cup	150 mL
Lemon juice	2 tbsp.	30 mL
Grated lemon zest	1 tbsp.	15 mL
Vanilla	1 tsp.	5 mL
All-purpose flour	2 1/4 cups	550 mL
Baking powder	2 tsp.	10 mL
Salt	1/2 tsp.	2 mL
LEMON GLAZE		
Icing (confectioner's) sugar	3/4 cup	175 mL
Water	2 tsp.	10 mL
Lemon juice	1 1/2 tsp.	7 mL

Gold or silver dragées (optional)

Cream margarine and sugar in large bowl. Add egg. Beat well. Add next 4 ingredients. Beat until smooth.

Combine flour, baking powder and salt in medium bowl. Add to margarine mixture in 2 additions, mixing well after each addition until no dry flour remains. Divide dough into 2 equal portions. Roll out 1 portion on lightly floured surface to 1/4 inch (6 mm) thickness. Cut out shapes with lightly floured 2 inch (5 cm) cookie cutter. Roll out scraps to cut more shapes. Arrange about 2 inches (5 cm) apart on greased cookie sheets. Bake in 350°F (175°C) oven for about 8 minutes until golden. Let stand on cookie sheets for 5 minutes before removing to wire racks to cool completely. Cool cookie sheets between batches. Repeat with remaining dough portion.

Lemon Glaze: Combine icing sugar, water and lemon juice in small bowl, adding more icing sugar or water if necessary until pourable consistency. Makes about 1/3 cup (75 mL) glaze. Brush glaze with small pastry brush on cookies.

Decorate with dragées. Let stand until set. Makes about 6 dozen (72) cookies.

1 cookie: 49 Calories; 1.7 g Total Fat (1 g Mono, 0.2 g Poly, 0.5 g Sat); 4 mg Cholesterol; 8 g Carbohydrate; trace Fibre; 1 g Protein; 47 mg Sodium

Pictured on page 41.

*These pretty cookies are so nice,
someone thought to name them twice!*

tip

To avoid over-handling, roll out cookie dough between 2 sheets of waxed or parchment paper. Over-handled dough will become tough and dry.

an added touch

Cut out centres with shaped cookie cutter appropriate for the occasion. For example, use a star or tree cookie cutter for Christmas, or a heart cookie cutter for Valentine's Day.

Jam Jams

Hard margarine (or butter), softened	1 cup	250 mL
Brown sugar, packed	1/4 cup	60 mL
Granulated sugar	1/4 cup	60 mL
Large eggs	2	2
Golden corn syrup	1/2 cup	125 mL
Vanilla	1 tsp.	5 mL
All-purpose flour	3 cups	750 mL
Baking powder	1/2 tsp.	2 mL
Salt	1/2 tsp.	2 mL
Apricot or raspberry jam (or jelly), approximately	3 tbsp.	50 mL
Icing (confectioner's) sugar, for dusting		

Cream margarine and both sugars in large bowl. Add eggs 1 at a time, beating well after each addition. Add corn syrup and vanilla. Beat until smooth.

Combine flour, baking powder and salt in medium bowl. Add to margarine mixture in 3 additions, mixing well after each addition until no dry flour remains. Roll out dough on lightly floured surface to 1/8 inch (3 mm) thickness. Cut out circles with lightly floured 2 1/2 inch (6.4 cm) round cookie cutter with fluted edge. Roll out scraps to cut more circles. Arrange about 2 inches (5 cm) apart on greased cookie sheets.

Cut out centres of 1/2 of circles with lightly floured 1 inch (2.5 cm) cookie cutter. Bake in 350°F (175°C) oven for 8 to 10 minutes until golden. Let stand on cookie sheets for 5 minutes before removing to wire racks to cool completely.

Spread about 1/2 tsp. (2 mL) jam on bottom of each whole cookie. Place cookies with cut-out centres on top of jam. Dust with icing sugar. Makes about 1 1/2 dozen (18) jam jams.

1 jam jam: 244 Calories; 11.5 g Total Fat (7.2 g Mono, 1.2 g Poly, 2.4 g Sat); 24 mg Cholesterol; 33 g Carbohydrate; 1 g Fibre; 3 g Protein; 224 mg Sodium

Pictured on page 43.

Sweet coconut macaroon topping on a pastry-like base. An interesting, delicious cookie!

about coconut

Such a lovely bunch of coconut! Fine or medium, flake or shredded (long thread), unsweetened or sweetened. Be sure to pay careful attention to which type the recipe requires as each provides a slightly different texture or sweetness.

Coconut Cookies

All-purpose flour	1 cup	250 mL
Baking powder	1/2 tsp.	2 mL
Salt	1/4 tsp.	1 mL
Hard margarine (or butter), softened	1/2 cup	125 mL
Egg yolks (large)	3	3
Milk	1 tbsp.	15 mL
COCONUT TOPPING		
Egg whites (large), room temperature	3	3
Icing (confectioner's) sugar	1 1/2 cups	375 mL
Shredded (long thread) coconut	2 1/2 cups	625 mL
Hard margarine (or butter), melted	1 tbsp.	15 mL

Combine flour, baking powder and salt in medium bowl. Cut in margarine until mixture resembles fine crumbs.

Beat egg yolks and milk with fork in small cup until well combined. Slowly add to flour mixture, stirring with fork until mixture starts to come together. Do not overmix. Form into flattened disk. Roll out dough on lightly floured surface to 1/4 inch (6 mm) thickness. Cut out circles with lightly floured 2 inch (5 cm) round cookie cutter with fluted edge. Roll out scraps to cut more circles. Arrange about 2 inches (5 cm) apart on ungreased cookie sheets.

Coconut Topping: Beat egg whites in large bowl until stiff peaks form. Add icing sugar in 2 additions, beating after each addition until smooth and glossy.

Fold in coconut and margarine. Makes about 1 1/2 cups (375 mL) topping. Spoon about 2 tsp. (10 mL) topping on top of each circle. Bake in 300°F (150°C) oven for about 30 minutes until golden. Remove to wire racks to cool. Makes about 2 1/2 dozen (30) cookies.

1 cookie: 133 Calories; 9.3 g Total Fat (2.8 g Mono, 0.5 g Poly, 5.4 g Sat); 22 mg Cholesterol; 12 g Carbohydrate; trace Fibre; 2 g Protein; 78 mg Sodium

Picture on page 45.

A little cookie with your coffee—a little coffee in your cookie!

Coffee Fingers

Hard margarine (or butter), softened	1 cup	250 mL
Brown sugar, packed	1/2 cup	125 mL
Egg yolk (large)	1	1
All-purpose flour	2 cups	500 mL
Icing (confectioner's) sugar	1/4 cup	60 mL
Instant coffee granules, crushed to fine powder	1 tsp.	5 mL
Egg white (large)	1	1
Finely chopped walnuts (or your favourite nuts)	1 1/2 cups	375 mL

Cream margarine and brown sugar in large bowl. Add egg yolk. Beat well.

Combine flour, icing sugar and crushed coffee granules in medium bowl. Add to margarine mixture in 2 additions, mixing well after each addition until no dry flour remains. Divide dough into 2 equal portions. Shape each portion into 6 inch (15 cm) long log. Roll out 1 log on lightly floured surface to 4 x 6 inch (10 x 15 cm) rectangle, about 1/2 inch (12 mm) thick. Cut into 1/2 x 2 inch (1.2 x 5 cm) rectangles.

Fork-beat egg white in small bowl.

Put walnuts into separate small bowl. Dip each rectangle in egg white until coated. Roll each in walnuts until coated, shaping into finger as you roll. Arrange about 2 inches (5 cm) apart on greased cookie sheets. Bake in 300°F (150°C) oven for 20 to 25 minutes until golden. Let stand on cookie sheets for 5 minutes before removing to wire racks to cool. Repeat with remaining log, egg white and walnuts. Makes about 4 dozen (48) fingers.

1 finger: 94 Calories; 6.5 g Total Fat (3.2 g Mono, 2 g Poly, 1 g Sat); 4 mg Cholesterol; 8 g Carbohydrate; trace Fibre; 2 g Protein; 50 mg Sodium

Pictured on page 47.

Get your fill of raisins with these scrumptious treats. Excellent with ice cream for dessert!

Raisin-Filled Cookies

RAISIN FILLING

Coarsely chopped raisins	1 1/4 cups	300 mL
Granulated sugar	1/2 cup	125 mL
Water	1/2 cup	125 mL
Cornstarch	2 tsp.	10 mL
Lemon juice	1 tsp.	5 mL
Hard margarine (or butter), softened	1 cup	250 mL
Granulated sugar	1 1/2 cups	375 mL
Large eggs	2	2
Vanilla	1 tsp.	5 mL
All-purpose flour	3 1/2 cups	875 mL
Baking soda	1 tsp.	5 mL
Salt	1/2 tsp.	2 mL

Granulated sugar, for decorating

Raisin Filling: Combine first 5 ingredients in medium saucepan. Bring to a boil on medium. Boil gently for 5 minutes, stirring occasionally. Remove from heat. Cool. Makes about 1 1/4 cups (300 mL) filling.

Cream margarine and second amount of sugar in large bowl. Add eggs 1 at a time, beating well after each addition. Add vanilla. Beat until smooth.

Combine flour, baking soda and salt in medium bowl. Add to margarine mixture in 3 additions, mixing well after each addition until no dry flour remains. Divide dough into 2 equal portions. Roll out 1 portion on lightly floured surface to 1/4 inch (6 mm) thickness. Cut out circles with lightly floured 2 1/2 inch (6.4 cm) round cookie cutter. Roll out scraps to cut more circles. Spread about 1 tsp. (5 mL) filling evenly on 1/2 of circles, leaving 1/4 inch (6 mm) edge. Place remaining circles on top of filling. Press edges together with fork to seal. Arrange about 2 inches (5 cm) apart on greased cookie sheets. Carefully cut 1/2 inch (12 mm) X in top of each cookie.

Sprinkle each cookie with third amount of sugar. Bake in 350°F (175°C) oven for about 10 minutes until golden. Let stand on cookie sheets for 5 minutes before removing to wire racks to cool. Repeat with remaining dough portion, filling and sugar. Makes about 3 dozen (36) cookies.

1 cookie: 161 Calories; 5.8 g Total Fat (3.6 g Mono, 0.6 g Poly, 1.2 g Sat); 12 mg Cholesterol; 26 g Carbohydrate; trace Fibre; 2 g Protein; 136 mg Sodium

Pictured on page 49.

Little pastry envelopes stuffed with a delightful filling.

pretty presentation

To create a visually impressive sweet tray, use varied shapes of cookies such as square, round or cut-out. For best eye-appeal, keep the cookies about the same size. Arrange them diagonally on the tray and choose a different shape for each row.

Sour Cream Nut Rolls

ALMOND FILLING

Ground almonds	2 1/2 cups	625 mL
Granulated sugar	1/2 cup	125 mL
Milk	1/4 cup	60 mL
Almond flavouring	1 tsp.	5 mL
All-purpose flour	2 cups	500 mL
Hard margarine (or butter), softened	1 cup	250 mL
Egg yolks (large)	2	2
Sour cream	1/2 cup	125 mL

Almond Filling: Combine first 4 ingredients in medium bowl. Makes 2 cups (500 mL) filling.

Measure flour into large bowl. Cut in margarine until mixture resembles fine crumbs.

Beat egg yolks and sour cream with whisk in small bowl until well combined. Slowly add to flour mixture, stirring with fork until mixture starts to come together. Do not overmix. Divide dough into 2 equal portions. Shape each portion into 6 inch (15 cm) long log. Flatten slightly. Roll out 1 log on lightly floured surface to 12 x 16 inch (30 x 40 cm) rectangle. Cut into 2 inch (5 cm) squares. Spoon about 1 tsp. (5 mL) filling across centre of each square. Fold diagonally opposite corners over filling. Pinch together to seal. Arrange about 2 inches (5 cm) apart on ungreased cookie sheets. Bake in 350°F (175°C) oven for 10 to 12 minutes until golden. Let stand on cookie sheets for 5 minutes before removing to wire racks to cool. Repeat with remaining log and filling. Makes about 8 dozen (96) rolls.

1 roll: 46 Calories; 3.3 g Total Fat (2 g Mono, 0.4 g Poly, 0.7 g Sat); 5 mg Cholesterol; 4 g Carbohydrate; trace Fibre; 1 g Protein; 25 mg Sodium

Pictured on page 51.

Lovely chocolate cookies sandwich a delectable chocolate filling accented with bourbon. Perfect for tea time.

variation

To make these cookies child-friendly, prepare the filling with 1 tsp. (5 mL) rum or brandy flavouring plus 2 tsp. (10 mL) water instead of using bourbon.

Bourbon Cookies

Hard margarine (or butter), softened	6 tbsp.	100 mL
Granulated sugar	1/4 cup	60 mL
Large egg	1	1
Golden corn syrup	2 tbsp.	30 mL
All-purpose flour	1 1/2 cups	375 mL
Cocoa, sifted if lumpy	1/4 cup	60 mL
Granulated sugar, for decorating		
BOURBON FILLING		
Semi-sweet chocolate chips	1/3 cup	75 mL
Bourbon whisky	1 tbsp.	15 mL
Icing (confectioner's) sugar	1 cup	250 mL
Hard margarine (or butter), softened	1/2 cup	125 mL

Cream margarine and first amount of granulated sugar in large bowl. Add egg. Beat well. Add corn syrup. Beat until smooth.

Combine flour and cocoa in small bowl. Add to margarine mixture in 2 additions, mixing well after each addition until no dry flour remains. Divide dough into 2 equal portions. Shape each portion into 6 inch (15 cm) long log. Flatten slightly. Roll out 1 log on lightly floured surface to 9 x 10 inch (22 x 25 cm) rectangle. Cut into 1 x 3 inch (2.5 x 7.5 cm) rectangles. Arrange about 2 inches (5 cm) apart on greased cookie sheets. Bake in 350ºF (175ºC) oven for 10 to 15 minutes until firm. Remove from oven.

Immediately sprinkle with second amount of granulated sugar. Let stand on cookie sheets for 5 minutes before removing to wire racks to cool completely. Repeat with remaining log and granulated sugar.

Bourbon Filling: Heat chocolate chips in small heavy saucepan on lowest heat, stirring often until almost melted. Do not overheat. Remove from heat. Stir until smooth. Cool to room temperature. Add bourbon. Stir.

Beat icing sugar and margarine in medium bowl until smooth. Add chocolate mixture. Beat well. Makes about 1 cup (250 mL) filling. Spread about 1/2 tbsp. (7 mL) filling on bottom of 1/2 of cookies. Place remaining cookies, sugar-side up, on top of filling. Makes about 2 1/2 dozen (30) cookies.

1 cookie: 115 Calories; 6.5 g Total Fat (3.9 g Mono, 0.6 g Poly, 1.6 g Sat); 7 mg Cholesterol; 14 g Carbohydrate; 1 g Fibre; 1 g Protein; 69 mg Sodium

Pictured on page 53.

These soft, old-fashioned cookies are a comforting snack. Great with a glass of milk any time!

Thick Molasses Cookies

Granulated sugar	1 cup	250 mL
Cooking oil	1 cup	250 mL
Large egg	1	1
Fancy (mild) molasses	1 cup	250 mL
Milk	1/2 cup	125 mL
Baking soda	2 tsp.	10 mL
All-purpose flour	5 1/2 cups	1.4 L
Salt	1/2 tsp.	2 mL

Beat sugar, cooking oil and egg in large bowl until thick and pale. Add molasses. Beat well.

Stir milk into baking soda in small cup until dissolved. Add to molasses mixture. Beat until smooth.

Combine flour and salt in separate large bowl. Add to molasses mixture in 3 additions, mixing well after each addition until no dry flour remains. Divide dough into 2 equal portions. Roll out 1 portion on lightly floured surface to 1/4 inch (6 mm) thickness. Cut out circles with lightly floured 2 1/2 inch (6.4 cm) round cookie cutter with fluted edge. Roll out scraps to cut more circles. Arrange about 2 inches (5 cm) apart on greased cookie sheets. Bake in 375°F (190°C) oven for 8 to 10 minutes until firm. Let stand on cookie sheets for 5 minutes before removing to wire racks to cool. Repeat with remaining dough portion. Makes about 5 dozen (60) cookies.

1 cookie: 109 Calories; 4.1 g Total Fat (2.3 g Mono, 1.2 g Poly, 0.3 g Sat); 4 mg Cholesterol; 17 g Carbohydrate; trace Fibre; 1 g Protein; 67 mg Sodium

Pictured on page 55.

Send them a kiss in their lunch boxes. Chocolate centres make these awesome blossoms look a bit like flowers.

tip

To keep decorated cookies in perfect shape during freezing, put completely cooled cookies back onto cookie sheets and freeze until firm before putting into airtight containers. Store in the freezer for up to 3 months.

Peanut Blossoms

Hard margarine (or butter), softened	1/2 cup	125 mL
Brown sugar, packed	1/2 cup	125 mL
Granulated sugar	1/2 cup	125 mL
Smooth peanut butter	1/2 cup	125 mL
Large egg	1	1
Milk	2 tbsp.	30 mL
Vanilla	1 tsp.	5 mL
All-purpose flour	1 3/4 cups	425 mL
Baking soda	1 tsp.	5 mL
Salt	1/2 tsp.	2 mL
Granulated sugar, approximately	1/3 cup	75 mL
Milk chocolate kisses, approximately	54	54

Cream margarine, brown sugar and first amount of granulated sugar in large bowl. Add peanut butter. Beat until well combined.

Add egg, milk and vanilla. Beat until smooth.

Combine flour, baking soda and salt in small bowl. Add to peanut butter mixture in 2 additions, mixing well after each addition until no dry flour remains. Roll into 1 inch (2.5 cm) balls.

Roll each ball in second amount of granulated sugar in same small bowl until coated. Arrange about 2 inches (5 cm) apart on ungreased cookie sheets. Bake in 375°F (190°C) oven for about 10 minutes until golden. Remove from oven.

Immediately place 1 chocolate kiss on top of each cookie. Press down until cookie cracks around edge. Let stand on cookie sheets for 5 minutes before removing to wire racks to cool. Makes about 4 1/2 dozen (54) cookies.

1 cookie: 90 Calories; 4.4 g Total Fat (2.2 g Mono, 0.6 g Poly, 1.4 g Sat); 5 mg Cholesterol; 12 g Carbohydrate; trace Fibre; 2 g Protein; 84 mg Sodium

Pictured on page 57.

With no flour and only three ingredients, the name pretty much says it all.

Easy Peanut Butter Cookies

Large egg	1	1
Granulated sugar	1 cup	250 mL
Crunchy peanut butter	1 cup	250 mL

Beat egg and sugar in medium bowl until thick and pale.

Add peanut butter. Beat until smooth. Cover. Chill for 1 hour. Roll into balls, using 1 tbsp. (15 mL) dough for each. Arrange about 2 inches (5 cm) apart on greased cookie sheets. Bake in 350°F (175°C) oven for 12 to 14 minutes until golden. Let stand on cookie sheets for 5 minutes before removing to wire racks to cool. Makes about 2 dozen (24) cookies.

1 cookie: 104 Calories; 5.9 g Total Fat (2.8 g Mono, 1.7 g Poly, 1.2 g Sat); 9 mg Cholesterol; 11 g Carbohydrate; 1 g Fibre; 3 g Protein; 58 mg Sodium

Pictured on page 59.

Delightfully decadent! Cranberries and white chocolate are a perfect pair.

Cranberry White Chocolate Cookies

Large eggs	2	2
Brown sugar, packed	1 3/4 cups	425 mL
Cooking oil	1/2 cup	125 mL
Vanilla	1 tsp.	5 mL
All-purpose flour	1 3/4 cups	425 mL
Baking powder	1 tsp.	5 mL
Baking soda	1/2 tsp.	2 mL
Dried cranberries	1 cup	250 mL
White chocolate chips	1 cup	250 mL

Beat eggs and brown sugar in large bowl until thick and pale. Add cooking oil and vanilla. Beat until smooth.

Combine next 3 ingredients in small bowl. Add to brown sugar mixture in 2 additions, mixing well after each addition until no dry flour remains.

(continued on next page)

Add cranberries and white chocolate chips. Mix well. Cover. Chill for 1 hour. Roll into balls, using 1 tbsp. (15 mL) dough for each. Arrange about 2 inches (5 cm) apart on greased cookie sheets. Bake in 375°F (190°C) oven for about 10 minutes until golden. Let stand on cookie sheets for 5 minutes before removing to wire racks to cool. Makes about 4 dozen (48) cookies.

1 cookie: 98 Calories; 3.8 g Total Fat (1.9 g Mono, 0.8 g Poly, 0.9 g Sat); 10 mg Cholesterol; 15 g Carbohydrate; 1 g Fibre; 1 g Protein; 31 mg Sodium

Pictured below.

Left: Easy Peanut Butter Cookies, page 58
Right: Cranberry White Chocolate Cookies, page 58

Kids will love these chocolatey treats. Perfect party fare.

Dirt Cups

COOKIE CUPS

Hard margarine (or butter), softened	1/4 cup	60 mL
Granulated sugar	1/2 cup	125 mL
Large egg	1	1
Vanilla	1/4 tsp.	1 mL
All-purpose flour	1 cup	250 mL
Cocoa, sifted if lumpy	3 tbsp.	50 mL
Salt	1/8 tsp.	0.5 mL

DIRT FILLING

Box of instant chocolate pudding powder (4 serving size)	1	1
Cold milk	1 cup	250 mL
Light sour cream	1/2 cup	125 mL
Gummy worms	24	24
Chocolate wafer crumbs	1/2 cup	125 mL

Cookie Cups: Cream margarine and sugar in medium bowl. Add egg and vanilla. Beat until smooth.

Combine flour, cocoa and salt in small bowl. Add to margarine mixture. Mix until no dry flour remains. Divide dough into 24 equal portions. Roll into balls. Press each ball into bottom and up side of greased mini-muffin cup. Bake in 350°F (175°C) oven for 8 to 10 minutes until firm. Let stand in pans on wire racks to cool slightly. Run knife around inside edge of each muffin cup to loosen. Remove cookie shells to wire racks to cool completely.

Dirt Filling: Beat pudding powder, cold milk and sour cream in separate medium bowl for about 1 minute until smooth. Makes about 2 cups (500 mL) filling. Spoon into each cookie shell.

Insert 1 gummy worm partway into filling in each shell. Sprinkle wafer crumbs over filling. Makes about 2 dozen (24) dirt cups.

1 dirt cup: 126 Calories; 3.3 g Total Fat (1.9 g Mono, 0.4 g Poly, 1.2 g Sat); 11 mg Cholesterol; 23 g Carbohydrate; trace Fibre; 2 g Protein; 129 mg Sodium

Pictured on page 61.

Top right: Dirt Cups, above
Bottom left: Egg Nests, page 62

Great any time, but especially cute for Easter.

Egg Nests

Oriental steam-fried noodles, broken up	3 cups	750 mL
Semi-sweet chocolate chips	1 cup	250 mL
Butterscotch (or peanut butter) chips	1 cup	250 mL
Jelly beans (your favourite), approximately	50	50

Measure noodles into large bowl.

Heat both chocolate and butterscotch chips in small heavy saucepan on lowest heat, stirring often until almost melted. Do not overheat. Remove from heat. Stir until smooth. Add to noodles. Stir until coated. Drop, using 1/3 cup (75 mL) for each, onto waxed paper-lined cookie sheets. Dent each in centre with thumb. Let stand until set. May be chilled to speed setting.

Put 5 jelly beans into each dent. Makes about 10 egg nests.

1 egg nest: 271 Calories; 10.3 g Total Fat (2.9 g Mono, 2.7 g Poly, 3.9 g Sat); 1 mg Cholesterol; 47 g Carbohydrate; 2 g Fibre; 2 g Protein; 74 mg Sodium

Pictured on page 61.

A spicy cookie made for dunking.

about ginger

Ground ginger is a hot, sweet spice derived from gingerroot. It is commonly used in Western cuisine to spice cakes and cookies. Gingerroot is more typically used in Asian cooking, and is not a substitute for ground ginger in baking.

Gingersnaps

Hard margarine (or butter), softened	3/4 cup	175 mL
Granulated sugar	1 cup	250 mL
Large egg	1	1
Fancy (mild) molasses	1/2 cup	125 mL
All-purpose flour	2 1/2 cups	625 mL
Baking soda	2 tsp.	10 mL
Ground ginger	2 tsp.	10 mL
Ground cinnamon	1 tsp.	5 mL
Salt	1/2 tsp.	2 mL
Granulated sugar, approximately	1/4 cup	60 mL

Cream margarine and first amount of sugar in large bowl. Add egg. Beat well. Add molasses. Beat until smooth.

(continued on next page)

Combine next 5 ingredients in medium bowl. Add to margarine mixture in 2 additions, mixing well after each addition until no dry flour remains. Roll into 1 inch (2.5 cm) balls.

Roll each ball in second amount of sugar in small bowl until coated. Arrange about 2 inches (5 cm) apart on greased cookie sheets. Bake in 350°F (175°C) oven for about 10 minutes until just firm. Let stand on cookie sheets for about 5 minutes before removing to wire racks to cool. Makes about 7 1/2 dozen (90) cookies.

*1 cookie: 45 Calories; 1.7 g Total Fat (1.1 g Mono, 0.2 g Poly, 0.4 g Sat); 2 mg Cholesterol;
7 g Carbohydrate; trace Fibre; 0 g Protein; 62 mg Sodium*

Pictured below.

These pretty Crinkles make their eyes twinkle with delight!

tip

Run out of baking powder? For 1 tsp. (5 mL) baking powder, substitute 1/4 tsp. (1 mL) baking soda plus 1/2 tsp. (2 mL) cream of tartar.

Chocolate Crinkles

Hard margarine (or butter), softened	1/4 cup	60 mL
Granulated sugar	2 cups	500 mL
Large eggs	3	3
Vanilla	2 tsp.	10 mL
Unsweetened chocolate baking squares (1 oz., 28 g, each), chopped	4	4
All-purpose flour	2 1/2 cups	625 mL
Baking powder	2 tsp.	10 mL
Salt	1/2 tsp.	2 mL
Icing (confectioner's) sugar, approximately	1 cup	250 mL

Cream margarine and granulated sugar in large bowl. Add eggs 1 at a time, beating well after each addition. Add vanilla. Beat until smooth.

Heat chocolate in small heavy saucepan on lowest heat, stirring often until almost melted. Do not overheat. Remove from heat. Stir until smooth. Add to margarine mixture. Beat well.

Combine flour, baking powder and salt in medium bowl. Add to chocolate mixture in 2 additions, mixing well after each addition until no dry flour remains. Roll into 1 inch (2.5 cm) balls.

Roll each ball in icing sugar in small bowl until coated. Arrange about 2 inches (5 cm) apart on greased cookie sheets. Bake in 350°F (175°C) oven for 10 minutes. Cookies will be soft. Let stand on cookie sheets for 5 minutes before removing to wire racks to cool. Makes about 8 dozen (96) cookies.

1 cookie: 48 Calories; 1.4 g Total Fat (0.6 g Mono, 0.1 g Poly, 0.5 g Sat); 7 mg Cholesterol; 9 g Carbohydrate; trace Fibre; 1 g Protein; 28 mg Sodium

Pictured on page 65.

Crisp, chocolate biscotti dotted with chewy cranberries. Dunk away!

about biscotti

Biscotti is an Italian term meaning "twice baked." The dough is first baked as a loaf, then sliced and baked again to become hard and crunchy. Biscotti is great dipped into coffee or tea, and makes an excellent gift.

Choco-Cran Biscotti

Dried cranberries	1 cup	250 mL
Orange juice	3 tbsp.	50 mL
All-purpose flour	2 cups	500 mL
Cocoa, sifted if lumpy	1/3 cup	75 mL
Baking powder	1 tsp.	5 mL
Salt	1/4 tsp.	1 mL
Hard margarine (or butter), softened	1/4 cup	60 mL
Granulated sugar	1/2 cup	125 mL
Large eggs	3	3

Combine cranberries and orange juice in small microwave-safe bowl. Cover. Microwave on high (100%) for about 1 minute, rotating dish at halftime if microwave does not have turntable, until cranberries are softened. Cool.

Combine next 4 ingredients in large bowl. Make a well in centre.

Cream margarine and sugar in medium bowl. Add eggs 1 at a time, beating well after each addition. Add cranberry mixture. Stir. Add to well. Mix until soft dough forms. Turn out onto lightly floured surface. Knead 6 times. Shape into 16 inch (40 cm) long log. Place on greased cookie sheet. Flatten slightly. Bake in 350°F (175°C) oven for 30 minutes. Let stand on cookie sheet for 10 to 15 minutes until cool enough to handle. Cut log diagonally with serrated knife into 1/2 inch (12 mm) slices. Arrange, cut-side down, about 2 inches (5 cm) apart on same cookie sheet. Bake in 275°F (140°C) oven for 10 to 12 minutes until golden. Turn slices over. Turn oven off. Let stand in oven for another 30 minutes until dry and crisp. Remove to wire racks to cool. Makes about 2 dozen (24) biscotti.

1 biscotti: 97 Calories; 3 g Total Fat (1.6 g Mono, 0.3 g Poly, 0.7 g Sat); 27 mg Cholesterol; 16 g Carbohydrate; 1 g Fibre; 2 g Protein; 73 mg Sodium

Pictured on page 68.

Nutty Biscotti

All-purpose flour	2 1/2 cups	625 mL
Flaked hazelnuts (filberts), toasted (see Note)	2/3 cup	150 mL
Baking soda	1 tsp.	5 mL
Salt	1/4 tsp.	1 mL
Hard margarine (or butter), softened	1/4 cup	60 mL
Granulated sugar	3/4 cup	175 mL
Large eggs	2	2
Egg white (large)	1	1
Hazelnut-flavoured liqueur (such as Frangelico), optional	1 tbsp.	15 mL
Vanilla	1 tsp.	5 mL

Combine first 4 ingredients in large bowl. Make a well in centre.

Cream margarine and sugar in medium bowl. Add eggs 1 at a time, beating well after each addition. Add egg white. Beat well.

Add liqueur and vanilla. Beat until smooth. Add to well. Mix until soft dough forms. Turn out onto lightly floured surface. Knead 6 times. Shape into 16 inch (40 cm) long log. Place on greased cookie sheet. Flatten slightly. Bake in 350°F (175°C) oven for about 30 minutes until golden. Let stand on cookie sheet for 10 to 15 minutes until cool enough to handle. Cut log diagonally with serrated knife into 1/2 inch (12 mm) slices. Arrange, cut-side down, about 2 inches (5 cm) apart on same cookie sheet. Bake in 275°F (140°C) oven for 10 to 12 minutes until golden. Turn slices over. Turn oven off. Let stand in oven for about 30 minutes until dry and crisp. Remove to wire racks to cool. Makes about 2 dozen (24) biscotti.

1 biscotti: 123 Calories; 4.7 g Total Fat (3.2 g Mono, 0.5 g Poly, 0.7 g Sat); 18 mg Cholesterol; 18 g Carbohydrate; 1 g Fibre; 3 g Protein; 110 mg Sodium

Pictured on page 69.

Keep these in a clear glass cookie jar beside your coffee maker. Then there will always be something ready to serve when a friend drops by for coffee.

note

To toast nuts, spread them evenly in an ungreased shallow pan. Bake in a 350°F (175°C) oven for 5 to 10 minutes, stirring or shaking often, until desired doneness.

chocolate-dipped nutty biscotti

Heat 3/4 cup (175 mL) semi-sweet chocolate chips in small heavy saucepan on lowest heat, stirring often until almost melted. Do not overheat. Remove from heat. Stir until smooth. Hold biscotti by the end and dip straight down into chocolate until 1 inch (2.5 cm) is coated. Place on waxed paper-lined cookie sheet. Let stand until set.

Pictured on page 69.

Photo legend, next page
(Clockwise from left)
Filbert Fingers, page 71
Choco-Cran Biscotti, page 66
Snickerdoodles, page 70
Chocolate-Dipped Nutty Biscotti, above
Nutty Biscotti, this page
Snickerdoodles, page 70

An old favourite. Simple cinnamon flavour makes them irresistible.

Snickerdoodles

Hard margarine (or butter), softened	1 cup	250 mL
Granulated sugar	1 1/2 cups	375 mL
Large eggs	2	2
All-purpose flour	2 1/2 cups	625 mL
Cream of tartar	2 tsp.	10 mL
Baking soda	1 tsp.	5 mL
Salt	1/4 tsp.	1 mL
Granulated sugar	2 tbsp.	30 mL
Ground cinnamon	2 tsp.	10 mL

Cream margarine and first amount of sugar in large bowl. Add eggs 1 at a time, beating well after each addition.

Combine next 4 ingredients in medium bowl. Add to margarine mixture in 2 additions, mixing well after each addition until no dry flour remains. Roll into 1 inch (2.5 cm) balls.

Combine second amount of sugar and cinnamon in small bowl. Roll each ball in cinnamon mixture until coated. Arrange about 2 inches (5 cm) apart on ungreased cookie sheets. Bake in 375°F (190°C) oven for about 10 minutes until golden. Let stand on cookie sheets for 5 minutes before removing to wire racks to cool. Makes about 4 1/2 dozen (54) cookies.

1 cookie: 82 Calories; 3.8 g Total Fat (2.4 g Mono, 0.4 g Poly, 0.8 g Sat); 8 mg Cholesterol; 11 g Carbohydrate; trace Fibre; 1 g Protein; 79 mg Sodium

Pictured on pages 68/69.

Filbert Fingers

Butter (not margarine), softened	1 cup	250 mL
Brown sugar, packed	3/4 cup	175 mL
Milk	2 tbsp.	30 mL
All-purpose flour	2 1/2 cups	625 mL
Ground hazelnuts (filberts)	1 cup	250 mL
Semi-sweet chocolate melting wafers	1/3 cup	75 mL

Cream butter and brown sugar in large bowl. Add milk. Beat until smooth.

Add flour in 2 additions, mixing well after each addition until no dry flour remains. Add hazelnuts. Mix well. Shape into 2 inch (5 cm) long logs, using 1 tbsp. (15 mL) dough for each. Arrange about 2 inches (5 cm) apart on ungreased cookie sheets. Bake in 375°F (190°C) oven for about 10 minutes until golden. Let stand on cookie sheets for 5 minutes before removing to wire racks to cool completely.

Heat chocolate wafers in small heavy saucepan on lowest heat, stirring often until almost melted. Do not overheat. Remove from heat. Stir until smooth. Transfer to small custard cup. Holding the centre of 1 log, dip 1/2 inch (12 mm) of 1 end straight down into chocolate. Repeat with opposite end. Place on waxed paper-lined cookie sheet. Repeat with remaining logs and chocolate. Let stand until set. May be chilled to speed setting. Makes about 4 dozen (48) fingers.

1 finger: 91 Calories; 5.5 g Total Fat (2.1 g Mono, 0.3 g Poly, 2.8 g Sat); 11 mg Cholesterol; 10 g Carbohydrate; trace Fibre; 1 g Protein; 43 mg Sodium

Pictured on page 68.

Fabulous hazelnut cookies to share with family and friends.

tip

An alternative to melting chocolate on the stovetop is to melt it in the microwave. Heat the chocolate in a small, uncovered microwave-safe bowl on medium-high (70%) for 30 seconds. Stir well. Repeat heating and stirring until chocolate is smooth and glossy. Never put a lid on melting chocolate. Condensation can develop and the water will cause the chocolate to seize.

A pretty thimble cookie with an inviting cherry centre.

Cherry Winks

Hard margarine (or butter), softened	3/4 cup	175 mL
Granulated sugar	1 cup	250 mL
Large eggs	2	2
All-purpose flour	2 cups	500 mL
Baking powder	1 tsp.	5 mL
Baking soda	1/2 tsp.	2 mL
Salt	1/2 tsp.	2 mL
Chopped pecans (or walnuts)	1 cup	250 mL
Chopped pitted dates (or raisins)	1 cup	250 mL
Cornflake crumbs	3 cups	750 mL
Maraschino cherries, halved and blotted dry, approximately	42	42

Cream margarine and sugar in large bowl. Add eggs 1 at a time, beating well after each addition.

Combine next 4 ingredients in medium bowl. Add to margarine mixture in 2 additions, mixing well after each addition until no dry flour remains.

Add pecans and dates. Mix well. Roll into 1 inch (2.5 cm) balls.

Roll each ball in cornflake crumbs in separate medium bowl until coated. Arrange about 2 inches (5 cm) apart on greased cookie sheets. Dent each with thumb. Place 1 cherry half in each dent. Press down lightly. Bake in 350°F (175°C) oven for 10 to 12 minutes until golden. Let stand on cookie sheets for 5 minutes before removing to wire racks to cool. Makes about 7 dozen (84) cookies.

1 cookie: 71 Calories; 2.9 g Total Fat (1.8 g Mono, 0.5 g Poly, 0.5 g Sat); 5 mg Cholesterol; 11 g Carbohydrate; 1 g Fibre; 1 g Protein; 83 mg Sodium

Pictured on page 73.

Golden cookies with refreshing lemon flavour. Perfect with a cup of tea.

tip

When a recipe calls for both lemon zest and juice, grate the lemon first, then juice it.

variation

Add 1 cup (250 mL) raisins to the dough. Mix well. Roll into balls and bake as directed.

Lemon Crackles

Hard margarine (or butter), softened	1/2 cup	125 mL
Brown sugar, packed	1/2 cup	125 mL
Granulated sugar	1/4 cup	60 mL
Large egg	1	1
Lemon juice	2 tbsp.	30 mL
Grated lemon zest	1 tbsp.	15 mL
All-purpose flour	1 1/2 cups	375 mL
Baking powder	1 tsp.	5 mL
Baking soda	1/2 tsp.	2 mL
Granulated sugar, approximately	1/4 cup	60 mL

Cream margarine, brown sugar and first amount of granulated sugar in large bowl. Add egg. Beat well. Add lemon juice and zest. Beat until smooth.

Combine flour, baking powder and soda in medium bowl. Add to margarine mixture in 2 additions, mixing well after each addition until no dry flour remains. Roll into 1 inch (2.5 cm) balls.

Roll each ball in second amount of granulated sugar in small bowl until coated. Arrange about 2 inches (5 cm) apart on ungreased cookie sheets. Bake in 350°F (175°C) oven for 10 to 15 minutes until golden. Let stand on cookie sheets for 5 minutes before removing to wire racks to cool. Makes about 4 dozen (48) cookies.

1 cookie: 53 Calories; 2.2 g Total Fat (1.4 g Mono, 0.2 g Poly, 0.5 g Sat); 4 mg Cholesterol; 8 g Carbohydrate; trace Fibre; 1 g Protein; 47 mg Sodium

Pictured on page 75.

Sometimes known as Mexican Wedding Cakes or Russian Tea Cakes, these make an attractive addition to a plate of sweets.

buried cherry balls

Prepare cookie dough as directed. Roll into balls. Drain and blot dry 66 maraschino cherries. Press 1 cherry into each ball. Re-roll each ball to completely cover cherry with dough. Bake as directed.

almond balls

Omit the vanilla and pecans. Use the same amounts of almond flavouring and ground almonds.

Exceptionally good—just crackerjack!

Pecan Balls

Hard margarine (or butter), softened	1 cup	250 mL
Icing (confectioner's) sugar	1/2 cup	125 mL
Vanilla	2 tsp.	10 mL
All-purpose flour	2 1/4 cups	550 mL
Ground pecans	1 cup	250 mL
Icing (confectioner's) sugar, approximately	1/2 cup	125 mL

Beat margarine, first amount of icing sugar and vanilla in large bowl until smooth.

Add flour in 2 additions, mixing well after each addition until no dry flour remains. Add pecans. Mix well. Roll into 1 inch (2.5 cm) balls. Arrange about 2 inches (5 cm) apart on ungreased cookie sheets. Bake in 325°F (160°C) oven for about 20 minutes until golden. Let stand on cookie sheets for about 5 minutes until cool enough to handle.

Roll each ball in second amount of icing sugar in small bowl until coated. Place on waxed paper-lined cookie sheets. Cool. Makes about 5 1/2 dozen (66) balls.

1 ball: 61 Calories; 4 g Total Fat (2.6 g Mono, 0.6 g Poly, 0.7 g Sat); 0 mg Cholesterol; 6 g Carbohydrate; trace Fibre; 1 g Protein; 34 mg Sodium

Pictured on page 77.

Crackerjack Cookies

Hard margarine (or butter), softened	1 cup	250 mL
Brown sugar, packed	1 cup	250 mL
Granulated sugar	1 cup	250 mL
Large eggs	2	2
Vanilla	2 tsp.	10 mL
All-purpose flour	1 1/2 cups	375 mL
Baking powder	1 tsp.	5 mL
Baking soda	1 tsp.	5 mL

(continued on next page)

Quick-cooking rolled oats (not instant)	2 cups	500 mL
Crisp rice cereal	2 cups	500 mL
Medium unsweetened coconut	1 cup	250 mL

Cream margarine and both sugars in medium bowl. Add eggs 1 at a time, beating well after each addition. Add vanilla. Beat until smooth.

Combine flour, baking powder and soda in small bowl. Add to margarine mixture in 2 additions, mixing well after each addition until no dry flour remains.

Add rolled oats, cereal and coconut. Mix well. Roll into 1 inch (2.5 cm) balls. Arrange about 2 inches (5 cm) apart on ungreased cookie sheets. Bake in 375°F (190°C) oven for 7 to 9 minutes until golden. Let stand on cookie sheets for 5 minutes before removing to wire racks to cool. Makes about 6 dozen (72) cookies.

1 cookie: 83 Calories; 3.9 g Total Fat (1.9 g Mono, 0.4 g Poly, 1.4 g Sat); 6 mg Cholesterol; 11 g Carbohydrate; trace Fibre; 1 g Protein; 66 mg Sodium

Pictured below.

Left: Crackerjack Cookies, page 76
Right: Pecan Balls, page 76

An attractive, sweet treat with a traditional flavour combination that's hard to beat!

sacher torte bites

Instead of cherries, fill each dent with apricot jam. Drizzle with chocolate as directed.

Black Forest Cookies

Hard margarine (or butter), softened	1 cup	250 mL
Box of instant chocolate pudding powder (4 serving size)	1	1
Large egg	1	1
All-purpose flour	2 cups	500 mL
Granulated sugar, approximately	1/4 cup	60 mL
Maraschino cherries, drained and blotted dry, approximately	66	66
Semi-sweet chocolate chips	1/2 cup	125 mL
Hard margarine (or butter)	3 tbsp.	50 mL

Beat first amount of margarine and pudding powder in medium bowl. Add egg. Beat well. Add flour in 2 additions, beating well after each addition until no dry flour remains. Roll into 1 inch (2.5 cm) balls.

Roll each ball in sugar in small bowl until coated. Arrange about 2 inches (5 cm) apart on greased cookie sheets. Dent each with thumb. Bake in 325°F (160°C) oven for 5 minutes. Remove from oven. Press dents again. Bake for another 10 minutes until firm. Let stand on cookie sheets for 5 minutes before removing to wire racks to cool.

Place 1 cherry in each dent.

Heat chocolate chips and second amount of margarine in small heavy saucepan on lowest heat, stirring often until chips are almost melted. Do not overheat. Remove from heat. Stir until smooth. Spoon chocolate into piping bag fitted with small writing tip or small resealable freezer bag with tiny piece snipped off corner. Drizzle small amount of chocolate mixture in decorative pattern over each cookie. Let stand until set. Makes about 5 1/2 dozen (66) cookies.

1 cookie: 70 Calories; 4 g Total Fat (2.4 g Mono, 0.4 g Poly, 1 g Sat); 3 mg Cholesterol; 8 g Carbohydrate; trace Fibre; 1 g Protein; 67 mg Sodium

Pictured on page 79.

Doubly delicious! Creamy filling and strawberry jam sandwiched between crisp cookies.

Strawberry Cream Cookies

Hard margarine (or butter), softened	3/4 cup	175 mL
Brown sugar, packed	1/2 cup	125 mL
Large egg	1	1
Vanilla	1/2 tsp.	2 mL
All-purpose flour	2 cups	500 mL
Baking powder	2 tsp.	10 mL
Baking soda	1/4 tsp.	1 mL
Salt	1/4 tsp.	1 mL
Medium unsweetened coconut	1/2 cup	125 mL
STRAWBERRY FILLING		
Icing (confectioner's) sugar	3/4 cup	175 mL
Hard margarine (or butter), softened	1/4 cup	60 mL
Strawberry jam	2 tbsp.	30 mL
Strawberry jam	1/4 cup	60 mL

Cream margarine and brown sugar in large bowl. Add egg. Beat well. Add vanilla. Beat until smooth.

Combine next 4 ingredients in medium bowl. Add to margarine mixture in 2 additions, mixing well after each addition until no dry flour remains. Add coconut. Mix well. Roll into balls, using 2 tsp. (10 mL) dough for each. Arrange about 2 inches (5 cm) apart on greased cookie sheets. Flatten with lightly floured fork to 1/4 inch (6 mm) thickness. Bake in 375°F (190°C) oven for 7 to 10 minutes until edges are golden. Let stand on cookie sheets for 5 minutes before removing to wire racks to cool.

Strawberry Filling: Beat icing sugar and margarine in small bowl until smooth. Add first amount of jam. Beat well. Makes about 1/2 cup (125 mL) filling. Spread about 1 tsp. (5 mL) filling on bottom of 1/2 of cookies.

Spread about 1/2 tsp. (2 mL) second amount of jam on bottom of remaining cookies. Sandwich cookies, using 1 cookie with filling with 1 cookie with jam. Makes about 2 dozen (24) cookies.

1 cookie: 175 Calories; 9.7 g Total Fat (5.4 g Mono, 0.9 g Poly, 2.9 g Sat); 9 mg Cholesterol; 21 g Carbohydrate; 1 g Fibre; 2 g Protein; 171 mg Sodium

Pictured on page 81.

These fancy little meringues are perfect with your after-dinner coffee. Elegantly dipped in chocolate.

Coffee Meringues

Egg whites (large), room temperature	2	2
Cream of tartar	1/2 tsp.	2 mL
Granulated sugar	1/3 cup	75 mL
Icing (confectioner's) sugar	1/3 cup	75 mL
Instant coffee granules	1 tbsp.	15 mL
Warm water	1 tbsp.	15 mL
Semi-sweet chocolate baking squares (1 oz., 28 g, each), chopped	4	4

Beat egg whites and cream of tartar in medium bowl on medium until soft peaks form. Add granulated sugar 1 tbsp. (15 mL) at a time, beating constantly until stiff peaks form and sugar is dissolved. Fold in icing sugar.

Stir coffee granules into warm water in small cup until dissolved. Fold into meringue. Spoon meringue into piping bag fitted with large plain tip. Pipe 1 inch (2.5 cm) diameter mounds, lifting tip to create pointed end on each, about 2 inches (5 cm) apart onto parchment paper-lined cookie sheets. Bake on bottom rack in 225°F (110°C) oven for 35 to 40 minutes until dry. Turn oven off. Let stand in oven until cooled completely.

Heat chocolate in small heavy saucepan on lowest heat, stirring often until almost melted. Do not overheat. Remove from heat. Stir until smooth. Transfer to small custard cup. Dip each meringue halfway into chocolate, allowing excess to drip back into cup. Place on same parchment paper-lined cookie sheets. Let stand until set. Do not chill. Makes about 4 dozen (48) meringues.

1 meringue: 21 Calories; 0.7 g Total Fat (0.2 g Mono, 0 g Poly, 0.4 g Sat); 0 mg Cholesterol; 4 g Carbohydrate; trace Fibre; 0 g Protein; 3 mg Sodium

Pictured on page 85.

Cream cheese makes these oh, so soft!

note

Sanding sugar is a coarse decorating sugar that comes in white and various colours and is available at specialty kitchen stores.

Spritz

Hard margarine (or butter), softened	1 cup	250 mL
Granulated sugar	1 cup	250 mL
Block of cream cheese, softened	4 oz.	125 g
Large eggs	2	2
Vanilla	1 1/2 tsp.	7 mL
Salt	1/4 tsp.	1 mL

(continued on next page)

All-purpose flour	3 cups	750 mL

DECORATING SUGGESTIONS
Dragées
Glazed cherries
Granulated sugar
Sanding (decorating) sugar (see Note)

Cream margarine and sugar in large bowl. Add cream cheese. Beat well. Add eggs 1 at a time, beating well after each addition. Add vanilla and salt. Beat until smooth.

Add flour in 3 additions, mixing well after each addition until no dry flour remains. Fill cookie press with dough. Press your favourite design(s) about 2 inches (5 cm) apart onto ungreased cookie sheets.

Decorate cookies as desired. Bake in 350°F (175°C) oven for 10 to 12 minutes until edges are just golden. Let stand on cookie sheets for 5 minutes before removing to wire racks to cool. Makes about 8 dozen (96) cookies.

1 cookie: 48 Calories; 2.6 g Total Fat (1.5 g Mono, 0.3 g Poly, 0.7 g Sat); 6 mg Cholesterol; 5 g Carbohydrate; trace Fibre; 1 g Protein; 35 mg Sodium

Pictured below.

chocolate spritz

Replace 6 tbsp. (100 mL) of the flour with 6 tbsp. (100 mL) of sifted cocoa. Prepare and bake as directed.

orange spritz

Omit the vanilla. Use 1/2 tsp. (2 mL) orange flavouring plus 2 tsp. (10 mL) grated orange zest. Prepare and bake as directed.

Delicate meringues bonded together with delicious lemon filling. Greet your family with "kisses"—they will love you for it!

tip

To easily fill a piping bag, set it point-down in a large glass. Fold the top of the bag over the top of the glass like a cuff. Spoon the mixture into the bag.

Lemon Meringue Kisses

LEMON FILLING

Water	1 tbsp.	15 mL
Cornstarch	1 1/2 tsp.	7 mL
Egg yolks (large)	2	2
Granulated sugar	1/4 cup	60 mL
Lemon juice	1/4 cup	60 mL
Hard margarine (or butter), cut up	1/4 cup	60 mL
Grated lemon zest	1 1/2 tsp.	7 mL

MERINGUE KISSES

Egg whites (large)	2	2
Cream of tartar	1/2 tsp.	2 mL
Granulated sugar	1/3 cup	75 mL
Icing (confectioner's) sugar	1/3 cup	75 mL

Lemon Filling: Stir water into cornstarch in small cup until smooth. Set aside.

Combine egg yolks and sugar in small heavy saucepan. Add lemon juice and margarine. Heat and stir on medium-low for 1 to 2 minutes until margarine is melted. Stir cornstarch mixture. Add to lemon mixture. Heat and stir for about 1 minute until boiling and slightly thickened. Remove from heat.

Add lemon zest. Stir. Transfer to small bowl. Cover with plastic wrap, placing it directly on surface to prevent skin from forming. Chill for about 2 hours, stirring occasionally, until cold. Makes about 3/4 cup (175 mL) filling.

Meringue Kisses: Beat egg whites and cream of tartar in medium bowl on medium until soft peaks form.

Add granulated sugar 1 tbsp. (15 mL) at a time, beating constantly until stiff peaks form and sugar is dissolved.

(continued on next page)

Fold in icing sugar. Spoon meringue into piping bag fitted with large plain tip. Pipe 1/2 inch (12 mm) high by 1 inch (2.5 cm) diameter mounds, lifting tip to create pointed end on each, about 2 inches (5 cm) apart onto parchment paper-lined cookie sheets. Bake on bottom rack in 225°F (110°C) oven for about 45 minutes until dry. Turn oven off. Let stand in oven until cooled completely. Spoon lemon filling into separate piping bag fitted with plain medium tip. Pipe about 2 tsp. (10 mL) filling onto bottom of 1 meringue. Press bottom of second meringue onto filling. Repeat with remaining meringues and filling. Makes about 2 dozen (24) meringue kisses.

1 meringue kiss: *53 Calories; 2.5 g Total Fat (1.5 g Mono, 0.3 g Poly, 0.7 g Sat); 18 mg Cholesterol; 7 g Carbohydrate; 0 g Fibre; 1 g Protein; 29 mg Sodium*

Pictured below.

Top: Lemon Meringue Kisses, page 84
Bottom: Coffee Meringues, page 82

Oodles of noodles make sweet, crunchy munchies! An old favourite.

Noodle Power

Semi-sweet chocolate chips	1 cup	250 mL
Butterscotch chips	1 cup	250 mL
Hard margarine (or butter)	1/4 cup	60 mL
Smooth peanut butter	1/4 cup	60 mL
Dry chow mein noodles	2 cups	500 mL
Unsalted peanuts	1 cup	250 mL

Heat first 4 ingredients in large heavy saucepan on lowest heat, stirring often until chocolate chips are almost melted. Do not overheat. Remove from heat. Stir until smooth.

Add noodles and peanuts. Stir until coated. Mixture will be soft. Drop, using 2 tsp. (10 mL) for each, onto waxed paper-lined cookie sheets. Let stand until set. May be chilled to speed setting. Makes about 3 dozen (36) cookies.

1 cookie: 102 Calories; 6.9 g Total Fat (3.1 g Mono, 1.6 g Poly, 1.8 g Sat); 0 mg Cholesterol; 10 g Carbohydrate; 1 g Fibre; 2 g Protein; 39 mg Sodium

Pictured on page 87.

Toffee with coffee—an afternoon treat.

Toffee Cookies

Bag of caramels (about 30)	9 1/2 oz.	269 g
Half-and-half cream	3 tbsp.	50 mL
Cornflakes cereal	2 cups	500 mL
Crisp rice cereal	1 cup	250 mL
Medium unsweetened coconut	1/2 cup	125 mL

Heat and stir caramels and cream in large saucepan on low for about 20 minutes until smooth. Remove from heat.

Add remaining 3 ingredients. Mix well. Drop, using 2 tsp. (10 mL) for each, onto greased cookie sheets. Let stand until set. May be chilled to speed setting. Makes about 3 1/2 dozen (42) cookies.

1 cookie: 41 Calories; 1.4 g Total Fat (0.1 g Mono, 0 g Poly, 1.1 g Sat); 1 mg Cholesterol; 7 g Carbohydrate; trace Fibre; 1 g Protein; 36 mg Sodium

Pictured on page 87.

Left: Toffee Cookies, above
Right: Noodle Power, this page

Make these whenever something sweet is in order. No cooking required!

Glazed Coffee Balls

Graham cracker crumbs	2 cups	500 mL
Icing (confectioner's) sugar	1/2 cup	125 mL
Finely chopped pecans	1/2 cup	125 mL
Hot water	1/2 cup	125 mL
Hard margarine (or butter)	2 tbsp.	30 mL
Instant coffee granules	1 tsp.	5 mL
COFFEE GLAZE		
Icing (confectioner's) sugar	3 cups	750 mL
Hard margarine (or butter), softened	3 tbsp.	50 mL
Cold prepared strong coffee	1/4 cup	60 mL
Finely chopped pecans (optional)		

Combine graham crumbs, icing sugar and pecans in medium bowl.

Stir hot water, margarine and coffee granules in 2 cup (500 mL) liquid measure until margarine is melted and coffee granules are dissolved. Add to crumb mixture. Mix well. Roll into 1 inch (2.5 cm) balls. Place on waxed paper-lined cookie sheets.

Coffee Glaze: Beat first 3 ingredients in small bowl, adding more icing sugar or coffee if necessary until barely pourable consistency. Makes about 1 1/2 cups (375 mL) glaze. Place 1 ball on top of fork. Dip into glaze until coated. Place on same waxed paper-lined cookie sheet. Repeat with remaining balls and glaze.

Sprinkle with pecans. Let stand until set. May be chilled to speed setting. Makes about 3 dozen (36) balls.

1 ball: 111 Calories; 3.6 g Total Fat (2.2 g Mono, 1.4 g Poly, 0.6 g Sat); 0 mg Cholesterol; 20 g Carbohydrate; trace Fibre; 1 g Protein; 53 mg Sodium

Pictured on page 89.

A saucepan cookie for peanut fans.
These won't last long.

Chocolate Peanut Drops

Granulated sugar	2 cups	500 mL
Milk	1/2 cup	125 mL
Hard margarine (or butter)	1/2 cup	125 mL
Cocoa, sifted if lumpy	6 tbsp.	100 mL
Smooth peanut butter	3/4 cup	175 mL
Vanilla	1 tsp.	5 mL
Quick-cooking rolled oats (not instant)	3 cups	750 mL
Chopped peanuts (or your favourite nuts), optional	1/2 cup	125 mL

Combine first 4 ingredients in medium saucepan. Bring to a boil on medium. Remove from heat.

Add peanut butter and vanilla. Stir until smooth. Add rolled oats and peanuts. Mix well. Let stand for 15 minutes. Working quickly, roll into small balls, using 1 tbsp. (15 mL) dough for each. Place on waxed paper-lined cookie sheets. Chill for 2 to 3 hours until firm. Makes about 5 dozen (60) cookies.

1 cookie: 84 Calories; 3.8 g Total Fat (2 g Mono, 0.8 g Poly, 0.8 g Sat); 0 mg Cholesterol; 12 g Carbohydrate; 1 g Fibre; 2 g Protein; 36 mg Sodium

Pictured on page 91.

Sweet and smooth, these taste like candy.
Everyone's sure to think they're dandy!

Peanut Butter Chip Balls

Smooth peanut butter	1 cup	250 mL
Semi-sweet chocolate chips	1 cup	250 mL
Sweetened condensed milk	1/2 cup	125 mL
Icing (confectioner's) sugar	1/2 cup	125 mL

Combine all 4 ingredients in medium bowl. Roll into 1 inch (2.5 cm) balls. Place on waxed paper-lined cookie sheets. Chill for 2 to 3 hours until firm. Makes about 3 1/2 dozen (42) balls.

1 ball: 77 Calories; 4.9 g Total Fat (2.1 g Mono, 1 g Poly, 1.6 g Sat); 1 mg Cholesterol; 8 g Carbohydrate; 1 g Fibre; 2 g Protein; 36 mg Sodium

Pictured on page 91.

Top: Peanut Butter Chip Balls, above
Bottom: Chocolate Peanut Drops, this page

These gently sweet treats are quick and easy to make.

note

To speed preparation, use a food processor to finely chop apricots and walnuts.

Apricot Balls

Medium unsweetened coconut	2 cups	500 mL
Very finely chopped dried apricot	1/2 lb.	225 g
Finely chopped walnuts (or your favourite nuts)	1/2 cup	125 mL
Sweetened condensed milk	1/2 cup	125 mL
Icing (confectioner's) sugar	1/4 cup	60 mL
Grated orange zest	1/2 tsp.	2 mL

Combine all 6 ingredients in medium bowl (see Note). Roll into 1 inch (2.5 cm) balls. Place on waxed paper-lined cookie sheets. Chill for 2 to 3 hours until firm. Makes about 5 dozen (60) balls.

1 ball: 47 Calories; 2.9 g Total Fat (0.3 g Mono, 0.5 g Poly, 2 g Sat); 1 mg Cholesterol; 5 g Carbohydrate; 1 g Fibre; 1 g Protein; 5 mg Sodium

Pictured on page 93.

Keep some of these on hand in the freezer for unexpected company. They'll be glad you did!

Cream Cheese Balls

Block of cream cheese, softened	8 oz.	250 g
Icing (confectioner's) sugar	1 cup	250 mL
Medium unsweetened coconut	1 cup	250 mL
Finely chopped maraschino cherries	1/3 cup	75 mL
Finely crushed vanilla wafers (about 80 wafers)	3 cups	750 mL
Can of crushed pineapple, drained	14 oz.	398 mL
GRAHAM CRACKER COATING		
Hard margarine (or butter)	2 tbsp.	30 mL
Graham cracker crumbs	3/4 cup	175 mL
Granulated sugar	1 tbsp.	15 mL

Beat cream cheese and icing sugar in large bowl until smooth. Add coconut and cherries. Stir.

Add crushed wafers and pineapple. Mix well. Cover. Chill for about 30 minutes until firm. Roll into 1 inch (2.5 cm) balls. Place on waxed paper-lined cookie sheets.

(continued on next page)

Graham Cracker Coating: Melt margarine in small saucepan on medium. Remove from heat. Add graham crumbs and sugar. Mix well. Roll balls in crumb mixture until coated. Place on same waxed paper-lined cookie sheet. Chill for 2 to 3 hours until firm. Makes about 7 dozen (84) balls.

1 ball: 46 Calories; 2.6 g Total Fat (0.7 g Mono, 0.2 g Poly, 1.5 g Sat); 5 mg Cholesterol; 5 g Carbohydrate; trace Fibre; 1 g Protein; 27 mg Sodium

Pictured below.

Left: Cream Cheese Balls, page 92
Right: Apricot Balls, page 92

Crisp, crunchy treats for the kid in each of us. Fabulous!

note

If chocolate becomes too thick for dipping, reheat on low until desired consistency.

Peanut Butter Balls

Smooth peanut butter	1 cup	250 mL
Icing (confectioner's) sugar	1 cup	250 mL
Hard margarine (or butter), softened	1 tbsp.	15 mL
Crisp rice cereal	1 cup	250 mL
Finely chopped walnuts	1/2 cup	125 mL
Chocolate melting wafers	2/3 cup	150 mL

Beat peanut butter, icing sugar and margarine in medium bowl until smooth.

Add cereal and walnuts. Mix well. Roll into 1 inch (2.5 cm) balls. Place on waxed paper-lined cookie sheets. Chill for 2 to 3 hours until firm.

Heat chocolate wafers in small heavy saucepan on lowest heat, stirring often until almost melted. Do not overheat. Remove from heat. Stir until smooth. Place 1 ball on fork. Dip into chocolate until coated, allowing excess to drip back into saucepan (see Note). Place on same waxed paper-lined cookie sheet. Repeat with remaining balls and chocolate. Let stand until set. May be chilled to speed setting. Makes about 4 1/2 dozen (54) balls.

1 ball: 62 Calories; 4.2 g Total Fat (1.7 g Mono, 1.2 g Poly, 1 g Sat); 0 mg Cholesterol; 5 g Carbohydrate; trace Fibre; 2 g Protein; 33 mg Sodium

Pictured on page 95.

The easiest recipe for first-time cooks to make. Maybe that's why this is such an old favourite! Simply delicious.

variation

Add a new twist to this classic cookie. Reduce the rolled oats to 1 1/2 cups (375 mL) and add 1 cup (250 mL) medium unsweetened coconut and 1/2 cup (125 mL) chopped glazed cherries.

Boiled Chocolate Cookies

Granulated sugar	2 cups	500 mL
Hard margarine (or butter)	1/2 cup	125 mL
Milk	1/2 cup	125 mL
Cocoa, sifted if lumpy	1/2 cup	125 mL
Quick-cooking rolled oats (not instant)	2 1/2 cups	625 mL

Combine first 4 ingredients in medium saucepan. Bring to a boil on medium. Reduce heat to medium-low. Simmer, uncovered, for 5 minutes, stirring occasionally. Remove from heat.

(continued on next page)

Add rolled oats. Mix well. Let stand for 15 minutes. Drop, using 1 tbsp. (15 mL) for each, onto waxed paper-lined cookie sheets. Chill for about 1 hour until firm. Makes about 5 1/2 dozen (66) cookies.

1 cookie: *56 Calories; 1.9 g Total Fat (1.1 g Mono, 0.3 g Poly, 0.4 g Sat); 0 mg Cholesterol; 10 g Carbohydrate; 1 g Fibre; 1 g Protein; 18 mg Sodium*

Pictured below.

Top: Boiled Chocolate Cookies, page 94
Bottom: Peanut Butter Balls, page 94

Laden with traditional Christmas ingredients, these will brighten any plate of goodies. Perfect for a cookie exchange.

tip

To keep logs of cookie dough from developing a flat side, turn them two or three times as they are chilling. Or, take a cardboard tube from a paper towel roll and cut it lengthwise. Put the wrapped log of cookie dough inside to maintain its round shape while chilling.

Merry Fruit Cookies

Coarsely chopped glazed cherries	2 cups	500 mL
Dark raisins	1 1/2 cups	375 mL
Chopped pitted dates	1 cup	250 mL
Red pineapple slices, cut up	4	4
Green pineapple slices, cut up	4	4
All-purpose flour	1/2 cup	125 mL
Hard margarine (or butter), softened	1 lb.	454 g
Granulated sugar	2 cups	500 mL
Large eggs	3	3
Vanilla	1 tsp.	5 mL
Almond flavouring	1/2 tsp.	2 mL
All-purpose flour	4 1/2 cups	1.1 L
Baking powder	1 tsp.	5 mL
Baking soda	1 tsp.	5 mL
Ground cinnamon	1/2 tsp.	2 mL

Put first 5 ingredients into large bowl. Add first amount of flour. Stir until fruit is coated.

Cream margarine and sugar in extra-large bowl. Add eggs 1 at a time, beating well after each addition. Add vanilla and flavouring. Beat until smooth.

Combine remaining 4 ingredients in separate large bowl. Add to margarine mixture in 3 additions, mixing well after each addition until no dry flour remains. Add fruit mixture. Mix well. Divide dough into 4 equal portions. Shape each portion into 10 inch (25 cm) long log. Wrap each log with waxed paper. Chill for at least 6 hours or overnight. Discard waxed paper from 1 log. Cut into 1/4 inch (6 mm) slices. Arrange about 2 inches (5 cm) apart on greased cookie sheets. Bake in 375°F (190°C) oven for about 10 minutes until golden. Let stand on cookie sheets for 5 minutes before removing to wire racks to cool. Repeat with remaining logs. Makes about 13 dozen (156) cookies.

1 cookie: 72 Calories; 2.5 g Total Fat (1.6 g Mono, 0.3 g Poly, 0.5 g Sat); 4 mg Cholesterol; 13 g Carbohydrate; trace Fibre; 1 g Protein; 40 mg Sodium

Pictured on page 97.

Mmm... pretty much says it all!

Shortbread

Butter (not margarine), softened	1 lb.	454 g
Brown sugar, packed (see Tip)	6 tbsp.	100 mL
Icing (confectioner's) sugar	6 tbsp.	100 mL
All-purpose flour	4 cups	1 L

DECORATING SUGGESTIONS
Sanding (decorating) sugar (see Note)
Glazed cherries, cut up
Candy sprinkles

Cream butter and both sugars in large bowl.

Add flour in 3 additions, mixing well after each addition until no dry flour remains. Knead dough in bowl if necessary to incorporate flour. Divide dough into 4 equal portions. Shape each portion into 6 inch (15 cm) long log. Wrap each log with waxed paper. Chill for at least 6 hours or overnight. Discard waxed paper from 1 log. Cut into 1/3 inch (1 cm) slices. Arrange about 2 inches (5 cm) apart on ungreased cookie sheets.

Decorate slices as desired. Bake in 325°F (160°C) oven for 12 to 15 minutes until edges are golden. Let stand on cookie sheets for 5 minutes before removing to wire racks to cool. Repeat with remaining logs. Makes about 8 dozen (96) cookies.

1 cookie: 59 Calories; 3.9 g Total Fat (1.1 g Mono, 0.2 g Poly, 2.4 g Sat); 10 mg Cholesterol; 6 g Carbohydrate; trace Fibre; 1 g Protein; 40 mg Sodium

Pictured on page 100.

Nutty Cherry Shortbread

Butter (not margarine), softened	1 lb.	454 g
Brown sugar, packed	2 cups	500 mL
All-purpose flour	3 1/2 cups	875 mL
Cornstarch	1/2 cup	125 mL
Coarsely chopped glazed cherries	1 cup	250 mL
Ground (or finely chopped) almonds	1 cup	250 mL

Cream butter and brown sugar in large bowl.

Combine flour and cornstarch in medium bowl. Add to butter mixture in 3 additions, mixing well after each addition until no dry flour remains. Knead dough in bowl if necessary to incorporate flour mixture.

Add cherries and almonds. Mix well. Divide dough into 4 equal portions. Shape each portion into 8 inch (20 cm) long log. Wrap each log with waxed paper. Chill for at least 6 hours or overnight. Discard waxed paper from 1 log. Cut into 1/4 inch (6 mm) slices. Arrange about 2 inches (5 cm) apart on ungreased cookie sheets. Bake in 375°F (190°C) oven for about 8 minutes until just golden. Let stand on cookie sheets for 5 minutes before removing to wire racks to cool. Repeat with remaining logs. Makes about 10 dozen (120) cookies.

1 cookie: 67 Calories; 3.4 g Total Fat (1.1 g Mono, 0.2 g Poly, 1.9 g Sat); 8 mg Cholesterol; 9 g Carbohydrate; trace Fibre; 1 g Protein; 33 mg Sodium

Pictured on pages 100/101.

There's no reason why shortbread can't dress up a bit for the holidays! A nice change from the ordinary.

Photo legend, next page

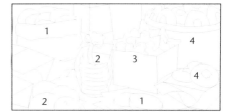

1. Nutty Cherry Shortbread, this page
2. Shortbread, page 98
3. Rolled Chocolate Shortbread, page 102
4. Whipped Shortbread, page 102

The chocolate you love in a buttery cookie. Yum.

variation

Enjoy the same great taste without fussing with cookie cutters! Shape each dough portion into 6 inch (15 cm) long log. Wrap each log with waxed paper. Chill for at least 6 hours or overnight. Discard waxed paper from 1 log. Cut into 1/4 inch (6 mm) slices. Bake as directed. Repeat with remaining log.

Rolled Chocolate Shortbread

Butter (not margarine), softened	1 cup	250 mL
Icing (confectioner's) sugar	1/2 cup	125 mL
Cocoa, sifted if lumpy	1/4 cup	60 mL
All-purpose flour	1 3/4 cups	425 mL

Beat butter and icing sugar in large bowl until smooth. Add cocoa. Beat well.

Add flour in 2 additions, mixing well after each addition until no dry flour remains. Knead dough in bowl if necessary to incorporate flour. Divide dough into 2 equal portions. Roll out each portion on lightly floured surface to 1/4 inch (6 mm) thickness. Cut out shapes with lightly floured 2 3/4 inch (7 cm) cookie cutters. Roll out scraps to cut more shapes. Arrange about 2 inches (5 cm) apart on ungreased cookie sheets. Bake in 325°F (160°C) oven for about 12 minutes until firm. Let stand on cookie sheets for 5 minutes before removing to wire racks to cool. Cool cookie sheets between batches. Repeat with remaining dough portion. Makes about 3 dozen (36) cookies.

1 cookie: 79 Calories; 5.6 g Total Fat (1.6 g Mono, 0.2 g Poly, 3.4 g Sat); 15 mg Cholesterol; 7 g Carbohydrate; trace Fibre; 1 g Protein; 55 mg Sodium

Pictured on page 101.

Melt-in-your-mouth goodness you'll crave year-round.

an added touch

For a bit of sparkle, sprinkle cookies with granulated sugar or sanding (decorating) sugar before baking. Sanding sugar is a coarse decorating sugar that comes in white and various colours and is available at specialty kitchen stores.

Whipped Shortbread

Butter (not margarine), softened	1 cup	250 mL
Granulated sugar	1/2 cup	125 mL
All-purpose flour	1 1/2 cups	375 mL
Cornstarch	1/4 cup	60 mL
Maraschino cherries, halved and blotted dry (optional)	18	18

Beat butter and sugar in medium bowl for about 5 minutes until light and creamy.

(continued on next page)

Combine flour and cornstarch in small bowl. Add to butter mixture in 2 additions, mixing well after each addition until no dry flour remains. Drop, using 1 tbsp. (15 mL) for each, about 2 inches (5 cm) apart onto ungreased cookie sheets.

If desired, put 1 cherry half in centre of each cookie. Bake in 375°F (190°C) oven for about 12 minutes until edges are just golden. Let stand on cookie sheets for 5 minutes before removing to wire racks to cool. Makes about 3 dozen (36) cookies.

1 cookie: 86 Calories; 5.9 g Total Fat (1.9 g Mono, 0.3 g Poly, 3.4 g Sat); 15 mg Cholesterol; 7 g Carbohydrate; trace Fibre; 1 g Protein; 56 mg Sodium

Pictured on page 101.

Chewy Cookie Clusters

Cornflakes cereal	3 cups	750 mL
Golden raisins	1 1/2 cups	375 mL
Shelled pistachios, toasted (see Note)	1 1/2 cups	375 mL
Sliced almonds, toasted (see Note)	1 cup	250 mL
Chopped red glazed cherries	1 cup	250 mL
Grated orange zest	1/2 tsp.	2 mL
Can of sweetened condensed milk	11 oz.	300 mL
Hard margarine (or butter), melted	2 tbsp.	30 mL

Combine first 6 ingredients in large bowl.

Add condensed milk and margarine. Mix well. Drop, using 2 tbsp. (30 mL) for each, about 2 inches (5 cm) apart onto parchment paper-lined cookie sheets. Bake in 350°F (175°C) oven for about 8 minutes until golden. Let stand on cookie sheets for 5 minutes before removing to wire racks to cool. Makes about 4 dozen (48) cookies.

1 cookie: 104 Calories; 4.7 g Total Fat (2.8 g Mono, 0.7 g Poly, 1 g Sat); 3 mg Cholesterol; 15 g Carbohydrate; 1 g Fibre; 2 g Protein; 33 mg Sodium

Pictured on page 105.

An assortment of tasty tidbits makes colourful clusters for tea time.

note

To toast nuts, spread them evenly in an ungreased shallow pan. Bake in a 350°F (175°C) oven for 5 to 10 minutes, stirring or shaking often, until desired doneness.

So not everyone loves fruitcake, but these are so good they might just change someone's mind!

Fruitcake Cookies

Mixed glazed fruit	2 cups	500 mL
Raisins	1 cup	250 mL
Chopped pitted dates	1 cup	250 mL
Chopped pecans	1 cup	250 mL
All-purpose flour	1/2 cup	125 mL
Hard margarine (or butter), softened	1/2 cup	125 mL
Granulated sugar	1 cup	250 mL
Large eggs	2	2
Vanilla	1 tsp.	5 mL
All-purpose flour	1 cup	250 mL
Baking soda	1/2 tsp.	2 mL
Ground cinnamon (optional)	1/4 tsp.	1 mL

Put first 4 ingredients into large bowl. Add first amount of flour. Stir until fruit is coated.

Cream margarine and sugar in separate large bowl. Add eggs 1 at a time, beating well after each addition. Add vanilla. Beat until smooth.

Combine second amount of flour, baking soda and cinnamon in small bowl. Add to margarine mixture. Mix until no dry flour remains. Add fruit mixture. Mix well. Drop, using 1 1/2 tbsp. (25 mL) for each, about 2 inches (5 cm) apart onto greased cookie sheets. Bake in 325°F (160°C) oven for 15 to 18 minutes until golden. Remove to wire racks to cool. Makes about 5 dozen (60) cookies.

1 cookie: 96 Calories; 3.3 g Total Fat (2 g Mono, 0.6 g Poly, 0.5 g Sat); 7 mg Cholesterol; 17 g Carbohydrate; 1 g Fibre; 1 g Protein; 37 mg Sodium

Pictured on page 105.

In cup: Fruitcake Cookies, above
On saucer: Chewy Cookie Clusters, page 103

Pretty cookies to accent a plate of sweets.

note

To toast coconut and nuts, spread them evenly in separate ungreased shallow pans. Bake in a 350°F (175°C) oven for 5 to 10 minutes, stirring or shaking often, until desired doneness.

Striped Corners

Hard margarine (or butter), softened	1 cup	250 mL
Icing (confectioner's) sugar	1 1/2 cups	375 mL
Large egg	1	1
All-purpose flour	3 cups	750 mL
Salt	1/4 tsp.	1 mL
Irish cream-flavoured powdered coffee whitener	1/3 cup	75 mL
Cocoa, sifted if lumpy	1 tbsp.	15 mL
Flake coconut, toasted (see Note)	2/3 cup	150 mL
Chopped sliced almonds, toasted (see Note)	2/3 cup	150 mL
Milk chocolate chips	1 cup	250 mL

Beat margarine and icing sugar in large bowl until smooth. Add egg. Beat well.

Combine flour and salt in medium bowl. Add to margarine mixture in 3 additions, mixing well after each addition until no dry flour remains. Divide dough into 2 equal portions.

Add coffee whitener and cocoa to 1 portion. Mix until evenly coloured. Shape into 16 inch (40 cm) long log. Flatten slightly. Shape remaining portion into 16 inch (40 cm) long log. Flatten slightly. Wrap each portion with plastic wrap. Chill for 2 hours. Discard plastic wrap from 1 portion. Roll out between 2 sheets of waxed paper to 4 x 24 inch (10 x 60 cm) rectangle. Repeat with remaining portion. Discard top sheet of waxed paper from both rectangles. Flip 1 rectangle onto the other, aligning edges of dough as evenly as possible. Press together. Discard top sheet of waxed paper. Roll up tightly from short side, jelly roll-style, using waxed paper as a guide. Roll should be about 3 1/2 inches (9 cm) in diameter. Wrap tightly with same sheet of waxed paper. Chill for at least 6 hours or overnight. Discard waxed paper. Cut into 1/4 inch (6 mm) slices. Cut each slice into 4 wedges. Arrange about 2 inches (5 cm) apart on ungreased cookie sheets. Bake in 400°F (205°C) oven for about 7 minutes until edges are just golden. Let stand on cookie sheets for 5 minutes before removing to wire racks to cool. Cool cookie sheets between batches.

(continued on next page)

Combine coconut and almonds in small dish. Heat chocolate chips in small heavy saucepan on lowest heat, stirring often until almost melted. Do not overheat. Remove from heat. Stir until smooth. Dip curved edge of each cookie in chocolate, then immediately into coconut mixture. Place on waxed paper-lined cookie sheet. Let stand until set. Makes about 5 1/2 dozen (66) cookies.

1 cookie: 92 Calories; 5.4 g Total Fat (2.7 g Mono, 0.5 g Poly, 1.9 g Sat); 4 mg Cholesterol; 10 g Carbohydrate; trace Fibre; 1 g Protein; 48 mg Sodium

Pictured below.

Watch their eyes sparkle with delight when you bring these to the table!

note

The irregularly shaped end pieces that are created when cookies are cut this way make a great snack. Consider them "diamonds in the rough" and save the perfect diamonds for company!

Mocha Diamonds

Hard margarine (or butter), softened	1 1/2 cups	375 mL
Brown sugar, packed	1 1/2 cups	375 mL
Instant coffee granules, crushed to fine powder	1 1/2 tsp.	7 mL
Almond flavouring	1 1/2 tsp.	7 mL
All-purpose flour	3 1/3 cups	825 mL
Baking powder	3/4 tsp.	4 mL
Salt	1/2 tsp.	2 mL
Milk chocolate bars (3 1/2 oz., 100 g, each), finely chopped	3	3
Chopped sliced almonds	3/4 cup	175 mL

Cream margarine and brown sugar in large bowl. Add coffee granules and flavouring. Beat until smooth.

Combine flour, baking powder and salt in medium bowl. Add to margarine mixture in 3 additions, mixing well after each addition until no dry flour remains.

Add chocolate and almonds. Mix well. Line greased 11 x 17 inch (28 x 43 cm) baking sheet with sides with parchment (not waxed) paper, extending paper 2 inches (5 cm) over long sides. Press dough evenly in baking sheet. Place sheet of waxed paper on top. Roll evenly with rolling pin. Discard waxed paper. Bake in 325°F (160°C) oven for about 30 minutes until golden. Let stand in baking sheet on wire rack for 20 minutes. While still warm, make 10 evenly spaced cuts lengthwise about 1 inch (2.5 cm) apart. Cut diagonally across lengthwise cuts to create small diamond shapes (see Note). Let stand in baking sheet on wire rack until cooled completely. Holding parchment paper, remove from pan. Re-cut if necessary. Discard parchment paper. Makes about 11 dozen (132) cookies.

1 cookie: *57 Calories; 3.3 g Total Fat (1.9 g Mono, 0.3 g Poly, 0.9 g Sat); 1 mg Cholesterol; 7 g Carbohydrate; trace Fibre; 1 g Protein; 40 mg Sodium*

Pictured on page 109.

Brimming with an assortment of fruit and nuts, these cookies are the perfect choice to announce the arrival of the holiday season.

Christmas Cookies

Hard margarine (or butter), softened	1 cup	250 mL
Brown sugar, packed	3/4 cup	175 mL
Large egg	1	1
All-purpose flour	1 1/4 cups	300 mL
Baking soda	1/2 tsp.	2 mL
Ground cinnamon	1/2 tsp.	2 mL
Salt	1/2 tsp.	2 mL
Chopped walnuts	1 cup	250 mL
Chopped Brazil nuts	1/2 cup	125 mL
Slivered almonds	1/2 cup	125 mL
Chopped pitted dates	1/2 cup	125 mL
Chopped glazed cherries	1/2 cup	125 mL
Glazed pineapple slices, chopped	2	2

Cream margarine and brown sugar in large bowl. Add egg. Beat well.

Combine next 4 ingredients in medium bowl. Add to margarine mixture. Mix until no dry flour remains.

Add remaining 6 ingredients. Mix well. Drop, using 1 1/2 tbsp. (25 mL) for each, about 2 inches (5 cm) apart onto greased cookie sheets. Bake in 350°F (175°C) oven for 10 to 12 minutes until golden. Remove to wire racks to cool. Makes about 4 dozen (48) cookies.

1 cookie: 112 Calories; 7.5 g Total Fat (3.9 g Mono, 2 g Poly, 1.3 g Sat); 4 mg Cholesterol; 10 g Carbohydrate; 1 g Fibre; 2 g Protein; 88 mg Sodium

Pictured on page 111.

Extra-special cookies for extra-special occasions. When only the best will do, these are sure to impress!

note

To toast nuts, spread them evenly in an ungreased shallow pan. Bake in a 350°F (175°C) oven for 5 to 10 minutes, stirring or shaking often, until desired doneness.

serving suggestion

The liquid from the cranberry mixture is too good to waste! Drizzle it over sliced fresh fruit, add a dollop of whipped topping, and serve with Cranberry Macadamia Mounds. Delicious!

Cranberry Macadamia Mounds

Dried cranberries	1 1/2 cups	375 mL
Orange juice	1/2 cup	125 mL
Orange-flavoured liqueur (such as Grand Marnier)	2 tbsp.	30 mL
All-purpose flour	3 cups	750 mL
Brown sugar, packed	1 1/2 cups	375 mL
White chocolate chips	1 cup	250 mL
Coarsely chopped macadamia nuts, toasted (see Note)	1 cup	250 mL
Baking powder	1 1/2 tbsp.	25 mL
Salt	1/2 tsp.	2 mL
Large egg	1	1
Buttermilk (or reconstituted from powder)	1 cup	250 mL
Hard margarine (or butter), melted	2/3 cup	150 mL
Grated orange zest	1 tbsp.	15 mL

Combine first 3 ingredients in small bowl. Let stand for 30 minutes, stirring occasionally. Drain, reserving liquid if desired (see Serving Suggestion).

Combine next 6 ingredients in large bowl. Make a well in centre.

Beat remaining 4 ingredients with whisk in separate small bowl. Add to well. Add cranberries. Stir until just moistened. Drop, using 1 1/2 tbsp. (25 mL) for each, about 2 inches (5 cm) apart onto greased cookie sheets. Bake in 375°F (190°C) oven for 10 to 12 minutes until just golden and wooden pick inserted in centre of cookie comes out clean. Let stand on cookie sheets for 5 minutes before removing to wire racks to cool. Makes about 6 dozen (72) cookies.

1 cookie: 90 Calories; 4.2 g Total Fat (2.6 g Mono, 0.3 g Poly, 1.1 g Sat); 4 mg Cholesterol; 12 g Carbohydrate; 1 g Fibre; 1 g Protein; 70 mg Sodium

Pictured on page 113.

A versatile dough to bake into a variety of shapes. We've included a few suggestions below. Have fun!

cookie ornaments

Instead of circles, cut out festive shapes with an assortment of cookie cutters such as stars, Christmas trees and gingerbread men. Make a hole with a drinking straw about 1/2 inch (12 mm) from the top edge of each cookie before baking. Decorate with candies, sprinkles or Royal Icing, page 116. Tie ribbon through each hole for hanging.

lollipop cookies

Prepare dough as directed. Roll into balls, using 1/3 cup (75 mL) for each. With a flat-bottomed glass, press each ball on lightly floured surface to 1/4 inch (6 mm) thickness. Place 1 round on top of 5 inch (12.5 cm) lollipop stick, covering 1 to 1 1/2 inches (2.5 to 3.8 cm) of stick. Press dough lightly onto stick. Repeat with remaining rounds and sticks, arranging about 2 inches (5 cm) apart on greased cookie sheets, alternating direction of sticks. Bake in 350ºF (175ºC) oven for 8 to 10 minutes until firm. Let stand on cookie sheets for 5 minutes before removing to wire racks to cool.

Rolled Ginger Cookies

Hard margarine (or butter), softened	1/4 cup	60 mL
Granulated sugar	1/2 cup	125 mL
Fancy (mild) molasses	1/2 cup	125 mL
Water	1/3 cup	75 mL
All-purpose flour	3 1/4 cups	800 mL
Baking soda	1 tsp.	5 mL
Ground ginger	1 tsp.	5 mL
Salt	1/2 tsp.	2 mL
Ground cinnamon	1/2 tsp.	2 mL
Ground cloves	1/4 tsp.	1 mL
Golden corn syrup	2 tbsp.	30 mL
Assorted candies, for decorating		

Cream margarine and sugar in large bowl. Add molasses and water. Beat until smooth.

Combine next 6 ingredients in medium bowl. Add to margarine mixture in 3 additions, mixing well after each addition until no dry flour remains. Roll out dough on lightly floured surface to 1/4 inch (6 mm) thickness. Cut out circles with lightly floured 2 inch (5 cm) cookie cutter. Roll out scraps to cut more circles. Arrange about 2 inches (5 cm) apart on greased cookie sheets. Bake in 350ºF (175ºC) oven for 8 to 10 minutes until firm. Let stand on cookie sheets for 5 minutes before removing to wire racks to cool. Cool cookie sheets between batches.

Measure corn syrup into small custard cup set in small heatproof bowl. Pour boiling water into bowl until halfway up side of custard cup. Let stand until corn syrup is warm. Brush corn syrup with small paintbrush on top of each cookie. Decorate with candies as desired. Place on waxed paper-lined cookie sheets. Let stand until set. Makes about 2 dozen (24) cookies.

1 cookie: 125 Calories; 2.2 g Total Fat (1.3 g Mono, 0.3 g Poly, 0.5 g Sat); 0 mg Cholesterol; 24 g Carbohydrate; 1 g Fibre; 2 g Protein; 132 mg Sodium

Pictured on page 115.

A very good, versatile cookie. Cut out and decorate shapes appropriate for the occasion. For a fun birthday party activity, have the kids decorate them to take home as party favours.

an added touch

For a bit of sparkle, sprinkle cookies with granulated sugar or sanding (decorating) sugar before baking. Sanding sugar is a coarse decorating sugar that comes in white and various colours and is available at specialty kitchen stores.

royal icing

Beat 2 2/3 cups (650 mL) icing sugar, 1/4 cup (60 mL) water and 2 tbsp. (30 mL) meringue powder in large bowl on medium until stiff peaks form. Add food colouring, if desired. Spread icing on cookies and decorate with candy sprinkles or dragées. If preferred, spoon icing into piping bag fitted with small writing tip or into small resealable freezer bag with tiny piece snipped off corner. Pipe icing in decorative pattern onto cookies.

Sugar Cookies

Hard margarine (or butter), softened	3/4 cup	175 mL
Granulated sugar	3/4 cup	175 mL
Large egg	1	1
Vanilla	1 tsp.	5 mL
All-purpose flour	2 cups	500 mL
Baking soda	1 tsp.	5 mL
Cream of tartar	1 tsp.	5 mL
Salt	1/4 tsp.	1 mL
Ground cardamom (optional)	1/4 tsp.	1 mL

Cream margarine and sugar in large bowl. Add egg. Beat well. Add vanilla. Beat until smooth.

Combine remaining 5 ingredients in small bowl. Add to margarine mixture in 2 additions, mixing well after each addition until no dry flour remains. Divide dough into 2 equal portions. Shape each portion into flattened disc. Wrap each with waxed paper. Chill for at least 6 hours or overnight. Discard waxed paper from 1 disc. Roll out dough on lightly floured surface to 1/8 inch (3 mm) thickness. Cut out circles with lightly floured 2 inch (5 cm) cookie cutter. Roll out scraps to cut more circles. Arrange about 2 inches (5 cm) apart on greased cookie sheets. Bake in 350°F (175°C) oven for about 10 minutes until edges are just golden. Let stand on cookie sheets for 5 minutes before removing to wire racks to cool. Cool cookie sheets between batches. Repeat with remaining disc. Decorate with Royal Icing, if desired. Makes about 7 dozen (84) cookies.

1 cookie: 35 Calories; 1.8 g Total Fat (1.2 g Mono, 0.2 g Poly, 0.4 g Sat); 3 mg Cholesterol; 4 g Carbohydrate; trace Fibre; 0 g Protein; 43 mg Sodium

Pictured on page 117.

Serve these Jack-O'-Lanterns at your next Halloween party. They're sure to be a smash!

note

Paste food colouring makes a bolder colour than liquid food colouring and is the best choice for these cookies in order to avoid thinning dough.

raisin sandwich cookies

Omit the food colouring. Instead of jack-o'-lantern faces, make a design of your choice using a knife or a small cookie cutter. Bake as directed.

Jack-O'-Lantern Cookies

RAISIN FILLING

Chopped dark raisins	1 1/2 cups	375 mL
Water	1/2 cup	125 mL
Granulated sugar	1/4 cup	60 mL
Hard margarine (or butter)	2 tsp.	10 mL
Lemon juice	2 tsp.	10 mL
Salt, sprinkle		
Hard margarine (or butter), softened	1 cup	250 mL
Granulated sugar	1 1/4 cups	300 mL
Large eggs	2	2
Milk	1 tbsp.	15 mL
Vanilla	1 tsp.	5 mL
All-purpose flour	2 cups	500 mL
Whole wheat flour	2/3 cup	150 mL
Baking powder	2 tsp.	10 mL
Salt	1/2 tsp.	2 mL
Ground cardamom	1/4 tsp.	1 mL

Orange paste food colouring (see Note)

Raisin Filling: Combine first 6 ingredients in medium saucepan. Bring to a boil on medium, stirring occasionally. Reduce heat to low. Simmer, uncovered, for 10 to 12 minutes, stirring occasionally, until thickened. Cool. Makes about 1 1/4 cup (300 mL) filling.

Cream second amounts of margarine and sugar in large bowl. Add eggs 1 at a time, beating well after each addition. Add milk and vanilla. Beat until smooth.

Combine next 5 ingredients in medium bowl. Add to margarine mixture in 2 additions, mixing well after each addition until no dry flour remains.

Add food colouring, a small amount at a time, kneading dough in bowl until colour is even and dough is bright orange. Divide into 2 equal portions. Shape each portion into flattened disc. Wrap each with waxed paper. Chill for at least 6 hours or overnight. Discard waxed paper from 1 disc. Roll out dough on lightly floured surface to 1/8 inch (3 mm) thickness. Cut out circles with lightly floured 2 1/2 inch (6.4 cm) round cookie cutter. Roll out scraps to cut more circles. Use knife to cut out faces on 1/2 of circles (see photo, page 120).

(continued on next page)

Spread about 1 1/2 tsp. (7 mL) filling on each whole circle, leaving 1/4 inch (6 mm) edge. Place faces on top of filling. Press edges together with fork to seal. Arrange about 2 inches (5 cm) apart on ungreased cookie sheets. Bake in 375°F (190°C) oven for 10 to 12 minutes until firm. Let stand on cookie sheets for 5 minutes before removing to wire racks to cool. Repeat with remaining disc and filling. Makes about 3 dozen (36) cookies.

1 cookie: 143 Calories; 6 g Total Fat (3.8 g Mono, 0.7 g Poly, 1.3 g Sat); 12 mg Cholesterol; 21 g Carbohydrate; 1 g Fibre; 2 g Protein; 124 mg Sodium

Pictured on page 120.

Almond Finger Cookies

Vegetable shortening (or lard), softened	1 cup	250 mL
Granulated sugar	1 cup	250 mL
Large egg	1	1
Almond flavouring	2 tsp.	10 mL
All-purpose flour	2 1/2 cups	625 mL
Baking powder	1 1/2 tsp.	7 mL
Salt	1/4 tsp.	1 mL
Ground almonds	3/4 cup	175 mL
Whole blanched almonds	48	48

Cream shortening and sugar in large bowl. Add egg and flavouring. Beat well.

Combine flour, baking powder and salt in medium bowl. Add to shortening mixture in 3 additions, mixing well after each addition until no dry flour remains. Knead dough in bowl until smooth.

Add ground almonds. Mix well. Divide dough into 8 equal portions. Divide each portion into 6 pieces. Shape each piece into 3 inch (7.5 cm) long log or finger. Arrange about 2 inches (5 cm) apart on greased cookie sheets. Squeeze each finger in centre to form knuckle. Press 1 whole almond on 1 end of each finger to form nail. Bake in 350°F (175°C) oven for 10 to 13 minutes until firm. Let stand on cookie sheets for 5 minutes before removing to wire racks to cool. Makes 4 dozen (48) cookies.

1 cookie: 97 Calories; 5.8 g Total Fat (2.7 g Mono, 1.2 g Poly, 1.3 g Sat); 4 mg Cholesterol; 10 g Carbohydrate; trace Fibre; 1 g Protein; 26 mg Sodium

Pictured on page 121.

Let these point the way to party fun. Sensationally spooky and good for a laugh—a Halloween howl, you might say.

witch's fingers

Knead green food colouring into dough until desired shade is reached. Use paste food colouring to make a bolder colour. Use only a few drops of liquid food colouring to make a softer colour. Prepare and bake as directed. For coloured nails, soak whole almonds for 30 minutes in a mixture of 1/4 cup (60 mL) water and 1/8 tsp. (0.5 mL) red or green paste food colouring. Let dry.

Pictured on page 121.

Photo legend, next page
Left: Jack-O'-Lantern Cookies, page 118
Right: Almond Finger Cookies, this page and Witch's Fingers, above

And you thought monsters only hid under the bed! Find some friendly ones peeking out from these whimsical, cake-like treats. Great for a birthday or Halloween party.

halloween black moons

Omit the chocolate pudding powder and candies. Use the same package size of vanilla pudding powder plus enough orange paste food colouring to make the filling a bright orange. Spread between cookie halves as directed.

Pictured on page 123.

Mud Monsters

Hard margarine (or butter), softened	1/2 cup	125 mL
Granulated sugar	1 cup	250 mL
Cocoa, sifted if lumpy	1/2 cup	125 mL
Large eggs	2	2
Vanilla	1 tsp.	5 mL
All-purpose flour	2 cups	500 mL
Baking soda	1 1/2 tsp.	7 mL
Baking powder	1/2 tsp.	2 mL
Salt	1/2 tsp.	2 mL
Milk	1 cup	250 mL
COOL CHOCOLATE FILLING		
Envelopes of dessert topping (not prepared)	2	2
Box of instant chocolate pudding powder (4 serving size)	1	1
Cold milk	1 1/2 cups	375 mL

Assorted candies, for decorating

Cream margarine and sugar in large bowl. Add cocoa. Beat well. Add eggs 1 at a time, beating well after each addition. Add vanilla. Beat well.

Combine next 4 ingredients in medium bowl. Add to margarine mixture in 3 additions, alternating with milk in 2 additions, beginning and ending with flour mixture, beating well after each addition. Drop, using 3 tbsp. (50 mL) for each, about 4 inches (10 cm) apart onto greased cookie sheets. Bake in 425°F (220°C) oven for about 10 minutes until puffed and firm. Let stand on cookie sheets for 5 minutes before removing to wire racks to cool completely.

Cool Chocolate Filling: Beat dessert topping, pudding powder and cold milk in separate large bowl for about 5 minutes until spreading consistency. Makes 2 2/3 cups (650 mL) filling. Slice each cookie in half horizontally. Spread 2 tbsp. (30 mL) filling on bottom half of each cookie. Cover with top halves. Press each cookie gently until small amount of filling oozes out between layers.

Press candies into filling to create "monster" faces (see photo). Makes about 2 dozen (24) cookies.

1 cookie: 170 Calories; 6.6 g Total Fat (3 g Mono, 0.6 g Poly, 2.6 g Sat); 19 mg Cholesterol; 26 g Carbohydrate; 1 g Fibre; 3 g Protein; 276 mg Sodium

Pictured on page 123.

Top left: Halloween Black Moons, this page
Bottom right: Mud Monsters, above

Throughout this book measurements are given in Conventional and Metric measure. To compensate for differences between the two measurements due to rounding, a full metric measure is not always used. The cup used is the standard 8 fluid ounce. Temperature is given in degrees Fahrenheit and Celsius. Baking pan measurements are in inches and centimetres as well as quarts and litres. An exact metric conversion is given on this page as well as the working equivalent (Metric Standard Measure).

Pans

Conventional – Inches	Metric – Centimetres
8 × 8 inch	20 × 20 cm
9 × 9 inch	22 × 22 cm
9 × 13 inch	22 × 33 cm
10 × 15 inch	25 × 38 cm
11 × 17 inch	28 × 43 cm
8 × 2 inch round	20 × 5 cm
9 × 2 inch round	22 × 5 cm
10 × 4 1/2 inch tube	25 × 11 cm
8 × 4 × 3 inch loaf	20 × 10 × 7.5 cm
9 × 5 × 3 inch loaf	22 × 12.5 × 7.5 cm

Oven Temperatures

Fahrenheit (°F)	Celsius (°C)	Fahrenheit (°F)	Celsius (°C)
175°	80°	350°	175°
200°	95°	375°	190°
225°	110°	400°	205°
250°	120°	425°	220°
275°	140°	450°	230°
300°	150°	475°	240°
325°	160°	500°	260°

Spoons

Conventional Measure	Metric Exact Conversion Millilitre (mL)	Metric Standard Measure Millilitre (mL)
1/8 teaspoon (tsp.)	0.6 mL	0.5 mL
1/4 teaspoon (tsp.)	1.2 mL	1 mL
1/2 teaspoon (tsp.)	2.4 mL	2 mL
1 teaspoon (tsp.)	4.7 mL	5 mL
2 teaspoons (tsp.)	9.4 mL	10 mL
1 tablespoon (tbsp.)	14.2 mL	15 mL

Cups

1/4 cup (4 tbsp.)	56.8 mL	60 mL
1/3 cup (5 1/3 tbsp.)	75.6 mL	75 mL
1/2 cup (8 tbsp.)	113.7 mL	125 mL
2/3 cup (10 2/3 tbsp.)	151.2 mL	150 mL
3/4 cup (12 tbsp.)	170.5 mL	175 mL
1 cup (16 tbsp.)	227.3 mL	250 mL
4 1/2 cups	1022.9 mL	1000 mL(1 L)

Dry Measurements

Conventional Measure Ounces (oz.)	Metric Exact Conversion Grams (g)	Metric Standard Measure Grams (g)
1 oz.	28.3 g	28 g
2 oz.	56.7 g	57 g
3 oz.	85.0 g	85 g
4 oz.	113.4 g	125 g
5 oz.	141.7 g	140 g
6 oz.	170.1 g	170 g
7 oz.	198.4 g	200 g
8 oz.	226.8 g	250 g
16 oz.	453.6 g	500 g
32 oz.	907.2 g	1000 g (1 kg)

Casseroles

Canada & Britain		United States	
Standard Size Casserole	Exact Metric Measure	Standard Size Casserole	Exact Metric Measure
1 qt. (5 cups)	1.13 L	1 qt. (4 cups)	900 mL
1 1/2 qts. (7 1/2 cups)	1.69 L	1 1/2 qts. (6 cups)	1.35 L
2 qts. (10 cups)	2.25 L	2 qts. (8 cups)	1.8 L
2 1/2 qts. (12 1/2 cups)	2.81 L	2 1/2 qts. (10 cups)	2.25 L
3 qts. (15 cups)	3.38 L	3 qts. (12 cups)	2.7 L
4 qts. (20 cups)	4.5 L	4 qts. (16 cups)	3.6 L
5 qts. (25 cups)	5.63 L	5 qts. (20 cups)	4.5 L

Tip Index

Recipe Index